Liaison Engagement Success

PRACTICAL GUIDES FOR LIBRARIANS

About the Series

This innovative series written and edited for librarians by librarians provides authoritative, practical information and guidance on a wide spectrum of library processes and operations.

Books in the series are focused, describing practical and innovative solutions to a problem facing today's librarian and delivering step-by-step guidance for planning, creating, implementing, managing, and evaluating a wide range of services and programs.

The books are aimed at beginning and intermediate librarians needing basic instruction/guidance in a specific subject and at experienced librarians who need to gain knowledge in a new area or guidance in implementing a new program/service.

About the Series Editor

The **Practical Guides for Librarians** series was conceived by and is edited by M. Sandra Wood, MLS, MBA, AHIP, FMLA, Librarian Emerita, Penn State University Libraries from 2014-2017.

M. Sandra Wood was a librarian at the George T. Harrell Library, the Milton S. Hershey Medical Center, College of Medicine, Pennsylvania State University, Hershey, PA, for over thirty-five years, specializing in reference, educational, and database services. Ms. Wood received an MLS from Indiana University and an MBA from the University of Maryland. She is a fellow of the Medical Library Association and served as a member of MLA's Board of Directors from 1991 to 1995.

Ellyssa Kroski assumed editorial responsibilities for the series beginning in 2017. She is the director of Information Technology at the New York Law Institute as well as an award-winning editor and author of 36 books including *Law Librarianship in the Digital Age* for which she won the AALL's 2014 Joseph L. Andrews Legal Literature Award. Her ten-book technology series, *The Tech Set* won the ALA's Best Book in Library Literature Award in 2011. Ms. Kroski is a librarian, an adjunct faculty member at Drexel and San Jose State University, and an international conference speaker. She has just been named the winner of the 2017 Library Hi Tech Award from the ALA/LITA for her long-term contributions in the area of Library and Information Science technology and its application.

Recent Books in the Series Include:

50. *Gaming Programs for All Ages in the Library: A Practical Guide for Librarians* by Tom Bruno

51. *Intentional Marketing: A Practical Guide for Librarians* by Carol Ottolenghi

Liaison Engagement Success

A Practical Guide for Librarians

Ellen Hampton Filgo and Sha Towers

PRACTICAL GUIDES FOR LIBRARIANS, NO. 76

ROWMAN & LITTLEFIELD
Lanham • Boulder • New York • London

Published by Rowman & Littlefield
An imprint of The Rowman & Littlefield Publishing Group, Inc.
4501 Forbes Boulevard, Suite 200, Lanham, Maryland 20706
www.rowman.com

6 Tinworth Street, London SE11 5AL, United Kingdom

British Library Cataloguing in Publication Information Available

Library of Congress Cataloging-in-Publication Data

Names: Filgo, Ellen Hampton, 1975– author. | Towers, Sha, author.
Title: Liaison engagement success : a practical guide for librarians / Ellen Hampton Filgo and Sha Towers.
Description: Lanham : Rowman & Littlefield, [2021] | Series: Practical guides for librarians ; 76 | Includes bibliographical references and index. | Summary: "This book prepares academic liaison librarians for successful engagement whether they are new to the profession, new to liaison librarianship, or part of a transitioning organization"—Provided by publisher.
Identifiers: LCCN 2021005831 (print) | LCCN 2021005832 (ebook) | ISBN 9781538144633 (paperback) | ISBN 9781538144640 (ebook)
Subjects: LCSH: Liaison librarians—Vocational guidance. | Liaison librarians—Professional relationships. | Subject specialist librarians. | Academic libraries—Relations with faculty and curriculum. | Academic libraries—Relations with faculty and curriculum—United States—Case studies.
Classification: LCC Z682.4.L44 F57 2021 (print) | LCC Z682.4.L44 (ebook) | DDC 020.92—dc23
LC record available at https://lccn.loc.gov/2021005831
LC ebook record available at https://lccn.loc.gov/2021005832

Contents

Acknowledgments

We are extremely grateful for the many librarians, who, while also working under trying circumstances (from home, while supervising school for their children, in masked and socially distanced offices, or while in quarantine or isolation), contributed such great stories of engaged liaison work with their communities. Their work inspires us and challenges us to keep innovating and improving.

Many thanks to our colleagues at the Baylor University Libraries, who have been a great source of encouragement for us as we have undertaken this project.

We would also like to express our thanks to Barbara Hampton—not just Ellen's mother, but a great writer and editor herself—who read over drafts of the book with a keen eye and practical suggestions.

Sha would like to thank his family for all their love and support. Ann, Carter, and Max, you keep me grounded, remind me not to take myself too seriously and to always enjoy the ride. I would also like to thank Ellen for the many conversations we've had that served as the seedbed for our thoughts and approaches on liaison engagement and the presentations and articles that resulted from that work, all of which has sparked the labor of love that resulted in this book.

Ellen would like to thank her Baylor Faculty Women's Writing Program group for their encouragement and fellowship. She also thanks Sha for being a great library mentor, collaborator, and friend. She is also grateful for her family: for Marc and Andy's love of reading, which makes her librarian mama's heart happy, and for Kelly, who is an unending source of love, support, and strength.

List of Contributors

Contributed stories can be read in the supplement at the publisher's website.
www.liaisonengagementsuccess.com

- Teaching Evidence-Based Practice in Physical Therapy—by Karen S. Alcorn, Massachusetts College of Pharmacy and Health Sciences University
- Chemistry Lotería—by Aida Almanza, Texas A&M University San Antonio
- STEM Librarians in the Triple Helix Mix—by Innocent Awasom, Texas Tech University
- Creating Artists' Statements—by Andi Back, University of Kansas
- Classical Virtual Reality—by Caitlin Bagley, Gonzaga University
- Collaborating across Campus to Support Interdisciplinary Field Experiences—by Jennifer Beach, Longwood University
- Providing Library Outreach to Artists—by Nimisha Bhat, Smith College
- Collaborating with the Office of Graduate Studies for a Graduate Research Showcase—by Roxanne Bogucka and Meryl Brodsky, University of Texas
- Becoming the Bloomberg Expert—by Afra Bolefski, University of Manitoba
- A Practical Story about Public Poetry—by Patricia Brown, Northwestern State University
- A Librarian Makes a Zine—by Jill Chisnell, Carnegie Mellon University
- Liaising Where They Live: Hosting Library Office Hours at the First-Generation Student Dorm—by Kristina Clement, University of Wyoming
- Transcending "Us" and "Them"—by Ameet Doshi, Georgia Institute of Technology
- Liaison Engagement through Art and Museum Visits—by Jenna Dufour, University of California, Irvine
- Partnering with Peer Mentors to Engage First-Year Composition Students—by Erin Durham, Zoe Hwang, and Elaine MacDougall, University of Maryland, Baltimore County
- Creating a Doctoral Support Center—by Amy Dye-Reeves, Texas Tech University
- Milestone Anniversaries Celebrating Authors—by Jeanne Ewert, University of Florida
- Connecting Research to the Community—by Kian Flynn, University of Washington

List of Figures
and Table

Figures

Table

Preface

Academic libraries in the twenty-first century are increasingly shifting focus from collections to services,[1] which situates academic liaison librarians in a position in which they are both informing their users as well as listening to their needs in order to share what services the library offers. Ultimately, the overarching model for liaison librarians is *engagement* with users. Jaguszewski and Williams describe it this way:

> An engaged liaison seeks to enhance scholar productivity, to empower learners, and to participate in the entire lifecycle of the research, teaching, and learning process.
>
> Engagement requires an outward focus. By understanding the changing needs and practices of scholars and students, librarians can help shape future directions for the library and advance the library's mission within the larger institution. Building strong relationships with faculty and other campus professionals, and establishing collaborative partnerships within and across institutions, are necessary building blocks to librarians' success.[2]

We have written this book for the academic liaison librarians, whether they are new to the profession of librarian or new to the role of liaison, who would like to learn about how to engage with their user communities. Every community is different, and a liaison who takes up the tasks of engagement will need to be committed to building relationships, being flexible, and listening well, to understand the community's needs and meet them.

We are two liaison librarians who are passionate about engagement and enjoy the kinds of collaborations and service innovations that come about when liaisons truly connect to their community of users. We have also led teams of liaison librarians, and we know that liaisons who have taken the time to get to know their faculty and students and are embraced by them will be able to provide better services to them. Knowing and engaging with your community means knowing their needs sometimes even before they ask. Conversely, it means that when a problem comes up that a community member can't solve, he or she will often look to the liaison librarian first. Engaged liaisons help raise the value of the services that the academic library provides to the university, which is why we are so enthusiastic about the work of liaison librarianship.

The first chapter of this book explains how liaison librarianship has evolved from being collections focused to being user focused over the past few decades, to a place where liaisons are now engaging with their communities at every point along the research life cycle. The second chapter helps librarians take a good look at their liaison communities to help them figure out how to get to know the people in them in a systematic and strategic way. The third chapter explores mindsets that are necessary to be a successful liaison. The fourth chapter explores a variety of strategies for creating positive connections with constituents.

Chapters 5 through 10 take an in-depth look at engagement through discipline-specific lenses for humanities, social sciences, STEM fields, arts, professional disciplines and nonacademic units, such as residence life or student services. We define each discipline area and describe their approaches to research and their information-seeking behaviors, and then explain a few key points that liaisons to these disciplines should keep in mind. In each chapter, we highlight stories from liaisons who are currently working in these areas that illustrate creative ways to engage with their communities. While every story might not be immediately applicable on your own campus in your context, we offer them here to inspire the same kind of creativity, innovation, thoughtfulness, risk taking, and passion demonstrated in the work of these liaisons. The stories can be read in full in the supplement at the publisher's website.

Chapter 11 focuses on collaborations and partnerships both inside and outside the library that can strengthen the work and results of liaisons. Chapter 12 explores issues and recommendations for those who are leading teams of liaisons, particularly in how to develop a framework for the type of work that they are doing. Chapter 13 concentrates on how the work of liaisons can be assessed and evaluated.

We hope that whatever your situation, you'll find ideas to help you grow as a liaison librarian. If this is new territory for you, this book will offer many ways to develop rewarding liaison work. Many of the ideas presented here are lessons learned, sometimes the hard way, over decades of liaison librarianship. If you're new to liaison work, we hope that throughout this book you find guidance and support for this challenging, but exciting journey. If you're a seasoned liaison veteran, you've likely picked up this book because you know that learning from others' experiences is extremely valuable and that no matter how many years you've been a liaison, creating time and space for development and growth is critically important. We trust that the ideas and stories that we and many other liaison librarians have shared here will be an opportunity to reflect on the work ahead of you and a source of encouragement.

Notes

1. Jennifer K. Frederick and Christine Wolff-Eisenberg, "Ithaka S+R US Library Survey 2019" (Ithaka S+R, April 2, 2020).

2. Janice Jaguszewski and Karen Williams, "New Roles for New Times: Transforming Liaison Roles in Research Libraries" (Association of Research Libraries, 2013), 4, http://conservancy.umn.edu/handle/11299/169867.

CHAPTER 1

History and Evolution of Liaison Librarianship

◉ Why Does It Matter?

WHETHER YOU ARE A LIBRARIAN new to the profession who is taking on a liaison role, or a seasoned liaison librarian taking a job at a new library, it is important to know about the context of your position within your library organization as well as where the liaison program at your library exists along liaison librarianship's evolutionary path. The way liaison librarianship has changed and grown over many decades, as described in this chapter, is not the story for each individual library, and you may find yourself in a liaison position at a library that is still stuck in an old model. Or you may find yourself at a library with an engaged liaison model alongside a few colleagues who may still cling to reference desk hours or the details of book ordering. Understanding where liaison librarianship as a whole has been, how it has evolved, and where it is going can be helpful for you in your role to advocate for change, new roles, and new services.

◉ Public Service Trends

The history of liaison librarianship is closely connected to public service trends in librarianship as a whole. For many decades, services provided to the public within libraries were offered with the reference desk as the center—the "organizational pattern for delivery of those services."[1] Because the reference desk was seen as a place that is available at all times and for all people, it provides a useful focus for librarians who strongly uphold the value of public service. At the traditional reference desk, librarians interacted with patrons from many departments, backgrounds, and levels of knowledge and ability to meet their information needs.

Shift in Reference Services

However, in the last few decades, the traditional reference desk has experienced a radical change.[2] In the mid to late 1990s, with the rise of internet technology, reference desk use declined precipitously, as users saw in the internet an ability to access information without the mediation of a librarian. Jerry Campbell, in a withering 1992 criticism of the reference desk, declared that "our users themselves are gradually changing; they are coming to expect something different. They want information quickly and they want it delivered to them."[3] To combat this, reference librarians began to implement a variety of services, such as roaming reference, virtual reference or mobile reference, trying to meet users at their point of need, often using some sort of new technology, but ultimately, it was the shift in user information-seeking behavior that ultimately brought about the transformation of the reference desk.[4] While it still remains in many academic libraries (perhaps rebranded as an "information desk" or "help desk" or merged with a fuller service "information commons"), it is no longer the hub of user services.

While on the surface, declining reference statistics may have been a major catalyst for the sea change in how public services are provided, in the 1980s and early 1990s, before the internet was pervasive, there was a movement for reforming reference services. This movement centered on a few issues, the first being the increase in services being offered (including robust information literacy instruction programs) without the increase in staffing. Another issue was the tensions present in trying to offer both subject-specific and generalist reference service as well as both in-depth research consultations and directional information. Finally, there was the ever-present issue of the quality and accuracy of reference information being provided.[5] The reference desk was already on shaky ground before the internet age radically changed its users.

In 2000, Myoung Wilson, in describing how the reference desk has been altered by the internet-enabled culture of library users, asserted that "only by identifying and forging a new relationship between users and reference librarians (both at the reference desk and beyond) can reference culture be recalibrated." This recalibration has now taken place through the shift in the profession to liaison librarianship. Liaison librarianship was relational at its core when originally conceived. In 1977, Laurence Miller first coined the term and defined it as "formal, structured activity in which professional library staff systematically meet with teaching faculty to discuss stratagems for directly supporting their instructional needs and those of their students."[6] Miller's liaisons were drawn from across the library, not just from public services, or from the ranks of the reference librarians, and during the early days of liaison programs, this was the norm. The purpose of the liaison program was to serve as a vehicle for communication between the library and its users, assuming questions about acquisitions, collections and requests for bibliographic instruction would be primary (as the reference desk was still the main location for research questions). However, as the reference services reform movement began and reference departments were restructured, many academic libraries began to implement liaison programs from the ranks of the reference librarians, many of whom were subject specialists and for whom there was a natural connection to departments and faculty.

⑥ Evolution of the Liaison Model

The development of liaison programs in academic libraries was first benchmarked in 1992, when the Association of Research Libraries (ARL) published a SPEC Kit on liaison services in ARL libraries.[7] The report, which surveyed ARL libraries and examined their liaison policies, revealed that "twice as many libraries (59%) reported liaisons in both technical and public services as reported having only public services liaisons (31%)" and that "collection development was stated to be the primary activity supported by liaison relations" in nearly three-fourths of the documents examined.[8] Indeed, while the main focus of these early liaison programs was to provide two-way communication between the library and the faculty, the reason for that communication was for the purpose of collection development.[9] Reference, instruction, faculty orientation, and other library services were a secondary component, and were not always carried out by the liaison, who instead served as a mediator between the faculty and the department or librarian who provided the service. Therefore, Miller, in describing early liaison work, could not stress more strongly that "a full-fledged liaison program can be a very severe test of communication within the library."[10] The collections focus of early liaison programs was also codified by the Reference and Adult Services Division of the American Library Association (ALA), when they defined liaison work as "the relationships, formal and informal, that librarians (in this instance, librarians with multiple responsibilities) develop with the library's clientele for the specific purpose of seeking input regarding the selection of materials."[11] While collection development responsibilities dominated early liaison programs, the conclusion of the 1992 SPEC Kit hinted at future changes: "Until recently the library collection has formed the focus of library activity. But as the physical collection becomes less central, the user is becoming the focus of library services. The role librarians are to have in this decentralized information environment could depend largely upon the effectiveness with which liaison librarians are able to monitor, anticipate, and respond to user's information needs."[12]

Indeed, as technological changes swept through academic libraries in the late 1990s, some began to reconsider the roles of liaison librarians, sensing the shift in how library users interacted with information, and suggesting a more active and engaging role for librarians.[13] Many libraries still staffed liaison programs from both technical and public services departments, although some reported that liaisons from technical service roles were not as comfortable offering research assistance or instruction,[14] just as instructing users in how to use these new technologies to access information became increasingly important.[15] Other libraries reconfigured the duties of their liaisons to incorporate only reference, instruction, and communication with assigned departments, relegating collection development to a smaller group of librarians.[16] It was during this time that Virginia Tech developed its "College Librarian" program, which, while not formally called a "liaison" program, was assigned all the familiar liaison roles (reference and research, instruction, collection development, and communication) to the librarians in the program, but heavily emphasized the reference and instruction aspects and appointed librarians from the reference department. Echoing earlier thoughts about library users and their relationship to technology, their argument for a program that "gives students and other users access to the services formerly sought at the reference desk" was based on "considerable evidence of user naiveté about the Internet."[17]

IMPORTANT DOCUMENTS IN THE HISTORY AND EVOLUTION OF LIAISON WORK

- "Liaison Services in ARL Libraries," ARL SPEC Kit #189 (1992).
- "Guidelines for Liaison Work," Liaison with Users Committee, Collection Development and Evaluation Section, Reference and Adult Services Division (1992).
- "Liaison Services," ARL SPEC Kit #301 (2007).
- "Guidelines for Liaison Work in Managing Collections and Services," Liaison with Users Committee, Collection Development and Evaluation Section, Reference and Users Association (2009)
- Research Library Issues, no. 265, Special Issue on Liaison Librarian Roles, ARL Publications (August 2009).
- "Librarian Position Description Framework," University of Minnesota Libraries (2009).
- "Engaging with Library Users: Sharpening our Vision as Subject Librarians for the Duke University Libraries," Duke University Libraries (2011).
- "New Roles for New Times: Transforming Liaison Roles in Research Libraries," ARL (2013).
- "Leveraging the Liaison Model: From Defining 21st Century Research Libraries to Implementing 21st Century Research Universities," Ithaka S+R (2014).

Throughout the 2000s, libraries continued to establish, grow, assess, and reorganize liaison programs. Even though the Reference and User Association published guidelines in 2009 about liaison work that continued to define the work of liaisons as collection development,[18] librarianship was cementing the move away from a focus on its collections to a focus on its users. In an effort to once again benchmark academic library liaison programs, ARL produced another SPEC Kit in 2007; the ARL report determined that "the largest group to shoulder liaison responsibilities is the public service librarians" and that "subject librarian" was nearly synonymous with "liaison librarian."[19] This shifting of liaison work can be seen clearly in a 2006 article called "Going Boldly beyond the Reference Desk: Practical Advice and Learning Plans for New Reference Librarians Performing Liaison Work" which assumed that most liaison work was going to be done by reference librarians. The authors stated,

> [T]raditionally, library outreach and liaison work have focused on collection development, but with many libraries facing shrinking budgets and rising costs for serials and databases, librarians may not find very many opportunities to interact with faculty this way. Increasingly, librarians must find creative ways to reach out to faculty through library instruction, customized class Web pages, and other types of specialized library services. In this age where Internet search engines compete heavily with libraries as prime in-

formation providers, liaison librarians must continually remind their clientele about the advantages of the library and the services they offer.[20]

Hinting at new roles to come for liaison librarians, the 2007 SPEC Kit documented services new to the liaison role, such as scholarly communication education, copyright advice, and digital project support.[21]

THE HISTORY AND EVOLUTION OF LIAISON LIBRARIANSHIP

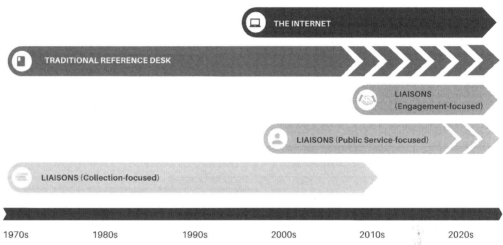

Figure 1.1. The history and evolution of liaison librarianship

⊚ Engaged Liaisons

ARL picked up the theme of new liaison roles and introduced new models of engagement with users in 2009 with a special issue of "Research Library Issues." The charge to liaison librarians: "new forms of relationship building, particularly with faculty, are central to effective liaison functions"[22] connecting "users with their information needs, whatever the format and whatever the technology."[23] This issue reported that liaisons who answered reference questions at a physical desk are now offering in-depth research consultations anywhere they may be needed—an office, in the academic department, or even virtually. Liaisons who taught library instruction classes are being embedded into the fabric of a course, creating assignments, joining them through learning management systems, and creating online tutorials and course pages. Liaisons who collected materials through firm ordering are jettisoning that role in favor of on-demand purchasing and selecting rarer items.

The change from focusing on collections to focusing on users brought on these new roles for liaisons. A collections focus was dedicated to the end-product of scholarship: the books, journals, and other documents that fill the shelves of the library. Focusing on users means engaging with them wherever they are and with whatever they are doing. Jaguszewski and Williams state it directly: "[A]n engaged liaison seeks to enhance scholar productivity, to empower learners, and to participate in the entire lifecycle of the research, teaching, and learning process."[24] This means that librarians are helping researchers create grant proposals, deposit their research data, and publish in open-access journals, as well as supporting digital scholarship projects and scaffolding information literacy into the curriculum of their departments.

Liaison programs have now evolved into a user-centered outreach and engagement arm of the library, connecting users with information and services. Because of their importance, it has become necessary for libraries with liaison programs to clearly define what liaison work means for their library.[25] In 2015, the third ARL SPEC Kit benchmarking liaison work described the services that liaisons are offering, which include the following:

- Primary services
  - departmental outreach
  - communication of departmental needs back to the library
  - reference
  - collection development
  - library instruction
  - scholarly communication education
- Additional services
  - assistance with scholarly impact and metrics
  - promotion of institutional repository
  - consultation on open-access issues
  - creating web-based learning objects
  - e-research support
  - data management support
  - consultation on intellectual property issues
  - new literacies education
  - data visualization support
  - GIS support
  - help with systematic reviews
  - text mining
  - promotion of open-access journal development[26]

The length of this list of services may seem daunting, but it does not rest on each individual liaison librarian's shoulders—it is only through a collaborative and flexible liaison program that users can be served so broadly.

While the primary services that today's liaison librarians offer to their users looks similar to the very early models of liaison librarianship, it is the focus on engaging with their users that listens to needs and adapts to meet them that has evolved the liaison model to where it is now.

Key Points

- Liaison librarianship has been a part of academic libraries for decades.
- Traditionally, it was a way to foster communication between academic departments and the library for the primary purpose of collection development.
- As academic libraries have shifted from being collections focused to being user focused, so has liaison librarianship.
- The focus of public service in academic libraries resides with the liaison librarians, rather than the reference desk.

- Today's liaison librarians offer a wide variety of services, connected to users' needs throughout the life cycle of research and teaching.
- Engaging with users is the key way to discover these needs.

⊚ Notes

1. Barbara J. Ford, "Reference beyond (and without) the Reference Desk," *College and Research Libraries* 47, no. 5 (1986): 491.

2. David A. Tyckoson, "Issues and Trends in the Management of Reference Services: A Historical Perspective," *Journal of Library Administration* 51, no. 3 (April 2011): 259–78, https://doi.org/10.1080/01930826.2011.556936.

3. Jerry D. Campbell, "Shaking the Conceptual Foundations of Reference: A Perspective," *Reference Services Review* 20, no. 4 (1992): 32, https://doi.org/10.1108/eb049164.

4. Myoung C. Wilson, "Evolution or Entropy? Changing Reference/User Culture and the Future of Reference Librarians," *Reference and User Services Quarterly* 39, no. 4 (2000): 387–90.

5. William Miller, "What's Wrong with Reference: Coping with Success and Failure at the Reference Desk," *American Libraries* 15, no. 5 (May 1984): 303–22; Ford, "Reference beyond (and without) the Reference Desk"; Campbell, "Shaking the Conceptual Foundations of Reference"; Peter Hernon and Charles R. McClure, "Unobtrusive Reference Testing: The 55 Percent Rule," *Library Journal* 111, no. 7 (1986): 37–41.

6. Laurence Miller, "Liaison Work in the Academic Library," *RQ* 16, no. 3 (April 1, 1977): 213.

7. Gail F. Latta, *Liaison Services in ARL Libraries. SPEC Kit 189* (Association of Research Libraries, 1992).

8. Latta, *Liaison Services in ARL Libraries.*

9. Marta A. Davis and M. Kathleen Cook, "Implementing a Library Liaison Program," *Collection Management* 20, no. 3–4 (July 15, 1996): 157–65, https://doi.org/10.1300/J105v20n03_14.

10. Miller, "Liaison Work in the Academic Library," 214.

11. Liaison with Users Committee, Collection Development and Evaluation Section, and Reference and Adult Services Division, "Guidelines for Liaison Work," *RQ* 32, no. 2 (1992): 198–204.

12. Latta, *Liaison Services in ARL Libraries.*

13. Tom Glynn and Connie Wu, "New Roles and Opportunities for Academic Library Liaisons: A Survey and Recommendations," *Reference Services Review* 31, no. 2 (June 1, 2003): 122–28, https://doi.org/10.1108/00907320310476594; Donald G Frank et al., "Information Consulting: The Key to Success in Academic Libraries," *The Journal of Academic Librarianship* 27, no. 2 (March 1, 2001): 90–96, https://doi.org/10.1016/S0099-1333(00)00180-4.

14. Cynthia C. Ryans, Raghini S. Suresh, and Wei-Ping Zhang, "Assessing an Academic Library Liaison Programme," *Library Review* 44, no. 1 (February 1995): 14–23, https://doi.org/10.1108/00242539510076961.

15. Carla A. Hendrix, "Developing a Liaison Program in a New Organizational Structure—A Work in Progress," *Reference Librarian* 32, no. 67/68 (February 28, 2000): 203–24, https://doi.org/10.1300/J120v32n67_15; Nancy H. Seamans and Paul Metz, "Virginia Tech's Innovative College Librarian Program," *College and Research Libraries* 63, no. 4 (July 2002): 324–32.

16. Hendrix, "Developing a Liaison Program in a New Organizational Structure—A Work in Progress."

17. Seamans and Metz, "Virginia Tech's Innovative College Librarian Program," 327.

18. Liaison with Users Committee, "Guidelines for Liaison Work in Managing Collections and Services," Reference and User Services Association, 2009, http://www.ala.org/rusa/resources/guidelines/guidelinesliaison.

19. Susan Logue et al., "Liaison Services, SPEC Kit 301 (October 2007)," October 1, 2007, 12, https://publications.arl.org/Liaison-Services-SPEC-Kit-301/.

20. Richard A. Stoddart et al., "Going Boldly beyond the Reference Desk: Practical Advice and Learning Plans for New Reference Librarians Performing Liaison Work," *The Journal of Academic Librarianship* 32, no. 4 (July 2006): 420, https://doi.org/10.1016/j.acalib.2006.03.009.

21. Logue et al., "Liaison Services, SPEC Kit 301 (October 2007)."

22. Karla Hahn, "Introduction: Positioning Liaison Librarians for the 21st Century," *Research Library Issues: A Bimonthly Report from ARL, CNI, and SPARC*, no. 265 (August 2009): 1.

23. Kara M. Whatley, "New Roles of Liaison Librarians: A Liaison's Perspective," *Research Library Issues: A Bimonthly Report from ARL, CNI, and SPARC*, no. 256 (August 31, 2009): 29.

24. Janice Jaguszewski and Karen Williams, "New Roles for New Times: Transforming Liaison Roles in Research Libraries" (Association of Research Libraries, 2013), 4, http://conservancy.umn.edu/handle/11299/169867.

25. Karen Williams, "A Framework for Articulating New Library Roles," *Research Library Issues: A Bimonthly Report from ARL, CNI, and SPARC*, no. 265 (August 31, 2009): 4–8; Anna Marie Johnson, "Connections, Conversations, and Visibility: How the Work of Academic Reference and Liaison Librarians Is Evolving," *Reference and User Services Quarterly* 58, no. 2 (January 18, 2019): 91–102, https://doi.org/10.5860/rusq.58.2.6929; Anne R. Kenney, "Leveraging the Liaison Model: From Defining 21st Century Research Libraries to Implementing 21st Century Research Universities" (Ithaka S+R, March 25, 2014), http://www.sr.ithaka.org/blog/leveraging-the-liaison-model-from-defining-21st-century-research-libraries-to-implementing-21st-century-research-universities/; See also the Baylor University Libraries' Liaison Framework, Sha Towers et al., "Liaison Framework for the Research and Engagement Librarians of Baylor University," Working Paper, accessed November 5, 2020, https://hdl.handle.net/2104/11086.

26. Rebecca K. Miller and Lauren Pressley, "Evolution of Library Liaisons, SPEC Kit 349," November 3, 2015, http://publications.arl.org/Evolution-Library-Liaisons-SPEC-Kit-349/.

Getting to Know Your User Community

THE MOST IMPORTANT ASPECT OF LIAISON WORK is getting to know your liaison areas. You need to determine who it is that makes up the community of people you are tasked with serving. In many ways the kind of engagement that will happen will be decided by the people who make up the departments, colleges, schools, and programs you are assigned to.

Getting to Know the People

It is important to acknowledge right from the beginning that you will not be able to form relationships with everybody in your community at the same level. There will be some people with whom you will have deeper relationships, some with whom you will only have superficial relationships, and some you may never meet. Even though that may be the case, at the very least you should still get to know your user community on paper: know names, research interests, and courses generally taught. However, there are always key people that you should make it a priority to meet.

Department Chair

Obviously, department chairs, as the main administrators, have significant influence over the department. They set budgets and allocate funds; they have a large part in hiring and evaluating faculty; they can even be on the frontline with students because at many institutions, they will often still teach a class or two, depending on the size of the department and institution. However, department chairs can also be under a lot of stress, as they serve as both an advocate for and a buffer between departmental faculty and higher administration. Having a chair on your side as the liaison can mean the full force of departmental authority on your side. In addition, because chairs work closely with their deans, having a good relationship with them could bring about the promotion of your work to the higher administration.

Undergraduate Program Directors

Every campus has different roles for their undergraduate program directors, but generally, these directors have a wide variety of oversight over the undergraduate curriculum of the department they serve. They often serve as a liaison to larger undergraduate curriculum administrative committees, submit any changes to courses or degree requirements, and review proposed new courses. Depending on their campus's advising structure, they may also advise student majors, or authorize substitutions for requirements in the department's major or minor programs. Undergraduate program directors can be important people to know as you work to integrate information literacy into the fabric of a curriculum, because they will have a broad knowledge of what is being taught in each course and where information literacy makes sense in the flow of the program as a whole. Often these positions are term-limited and may rotate among faculty members, so it's good to be aware of who is serving in that role. It is also important to figure out how much autonomy the particular undergraduate program director has in decisions compared with the departmental chair.

> I (Ellen) am very close with a faculty member in one of my liaison departments. We got to know each other when our children attended the same daycare and over time not only have our children become good friends, but so have our whole families. He became the undergraduate program director for his department a few years ago and one of his first tasks was to create a New Student Experience course for their first-year majors. He brought me in from the beginning of his planning and now every fall I am invited to the class to introduce myself as the department's librarian, explain the wealth of library resources for their discipline, and teach them about the Zotero citation management tool.

Graduate Program Director

Similar to the undergraduate program director, the graduate program directors oversee the graduate activities in the department. This may include responsibilities such as managing admissions to the program, allocating funding to the students, and running comprehensive exams, as well as administering the academic program and curriculum as a whole. They will also work with faculty advisors to monitor graduate students progress through the program. They often serve as mediator and advisor to the graduate students to resolve any problems that occur during their time in the program. Graduate program directors are important to get to know because they will be familiar with the graduate students' research needs. Graduate students are often both great users of and allies for the library, and liaisons who are on good terms with the graduate program director will be able to easily introduce themselves and their services to these key students.

Departmental Administrative Staff

It's entirely possible we should have listed these significant people first. Departmental administrative staff can make your liaison work run much more smoothly. They are the communication centers of the department, and communication is key to departmental engagement. They can give you access to email lists, provide key information about departmental dates and deadlines, or post your library-related information on departmental bulletin boards. They may also be the gatekeeper of the department chair's schedule, and so can be instrumental in helping you form that crucial relationship.

Other Support Staff

Depending on your liaison department, these people might have all sorts of titles. For instance:

- Lab coordinator
- Lab machinist
- Media center director
- Technology support
- Grant manager
- Research coordinator
- Coordinator of student recruitment
- Writing center director

While the titles may vary, the important thing to note here is that these are usually all roles that faculty rely on to do their jobs well. Knowing these people and having them be an advocate for your role as liaison librarian and the services that you can provide is crucial.

New Faculty

It is important to meet new faculty each year. First of all, they will most likely have research and teaching resource needs in areas new to the library, requiring purchases of books, journals, databases, or primary source materials. It is important to learn about those needs. However, meeting them is also important for introducing yourself, the library, and library resources and services into their newly forming habits at your institution. When you introduce yourself to them, they may or may not already have ideas about how a librarian fits into their teaching plan for the year, but if you are able to work with their class early on, it is more likely that your services will be considered as a part of their planning in the future. If the new faculty at your institution have an orientation program, and the library is not already a part of that, work with your administration on getting time during the orientation for all the liaison librarians to introduce themselves. At Baylor University, where we work, the library dean has an hour-long session during the new faculty orientation to talk about the libraries and services and to introduce the liaison librarians. The time that follows has traditionally been a break where the liaisons are encouraged to mingle with the new faculty, introducing themselves, handing out cards, and answering any initial questions they may have.

Pretenure Faculty

Getting to know pretenure faculty is an extension of getting to know new faculty, as many new faculty will be hired at the assistant professor level. Generally, this is a reminder that getting to know faculty isn't done with one meeting. Keep in touch with these faculty and keep nurturing your relationship with them as they progress toward tenure, with all of its pressures to research and publish. Pretenure faculty can be very busy and stressed, but you never know when contact with them might be beneficial as they progress toward their goals.

Master Teachers

Institutions of higher education, whether four-year liberal arts colleges or research-intensive universities with graduate programs, are at their core places where teaching happens. Many institutions recognize teachers with special designations for distinction in teaching. Whether they are called "master teachers" or "distinguished teachers" or they have won teaching awards that are chosen by a committee of their peers or are nominated by students, these faculty members have demonstrated excellence in the craft of teaching. These teachers are often open to discussing information literacy instruction and how it can be woven into their classrooms, because of an innate habit of reflecting on and trying to improve their own teaching practices.

Research Stars

Whether there is a formal designation by a research office, departments often have outstanding researchers, who have brought in many research dollars, published prolifically, or who have been noted for their scholarship by disciplinary associations. Sometimes it can be daunting to approach these scholars because of their aura of confidence, but even researchers who have been highly successful need help sometimes, whether it is with a literature review in an area new to them, learning digital scholarship tools they had previously never used, or setting up citation management systems after a lifetime of using a written notecard system. Creating relationships with these faculty researchers can be strategic because of the status their productivity bestows on them.

⑥ Getting to Know the Network

Although it is important to cultivate relationships with the people in the roles listed here, that does not mean that you should ignore everyone else. Put your political glasses on as you get to know your departments. Does the department contain factions that are disagreeing? Is there a faculty member who serves as a neutral figure or mediator in the department? Is the key figure in the department one who doesn't have any formal titles, but still seems to control the decisions? Is there someone who doesn't publish a lot, but who quietly serves on lots of committees and gets departmental work done? These people can also be important to get to know, although keep in mind that it is often beneficial to position the library above departmental mudslinging. You want to get to know the departmental politics, not become a part of it. We mention these other departmental characters because sometimes your entrée into the department can come from a surprising place. Your engagement with the department may seem to be failing until you meet that one particular person with influence, and with her or him on your side, doors suddenly start to open for you.

Getting to know an influential person in the department can open up relationships with a whole network of people. It is good to remember that relationships are not just one-to-one, but are woven into a network. Networking is "a critical key to building successful relationships. . . . [It] hinges on finding connections and making those connections apparent to all concerned."[1] Understanding how to network is crucial to building a base of support in a department. If you have a good interaction with a faculty member (whether that's a research consultation or an instruction session), she will tell her network of colleagues who are close to her about how it went. If that good interaction was with an influential department member, your reach might be even greater.

It may seem hard to keep track of the people in your departments, though. If the thought of it overwhelms you, you may want to try the method that one librarian gleaned from the development and fundraising world, where he tracked on an Excel spreadsheet the action steps he took with each faculty individually, in a way that was "appropriate to the status of the relationship, that is useful to their scholarly productivity, and that builds toward the next step of engagement."[2] Other libraries have begun to adopt customer relationship management software, such as LibCRM or Salesforce, to track engagement with liaison departments. (We will go into more detail on this in chapter 13).

⑥ Getting to Know Their Research

Understanding the research agendas of the faculty in your departments is vital to being able to offer proactive research assistance. If you know, for example, that a particular faculty member researches in a niche field, the next time a related article comes across your social media feed, or you bump into a new article or book related to the topic, you can send it to him with a note, asking whether he had seen it yet. In our experience, faculty members rarely become annoyed because you sent them information unsolicited—usually it is the opposite: they appreciate that you have been thinking of them and their interests. There are many ways to get to know the research of your faculty, including by reading their publications or attending their departmental lectures or colloquia, but the first and best way to learn is to ask them! Faculty love to talk about their research. A good starting question is, "So what are you working on?"

QUESTIONS TO ASK FACULTY ABOUT THEIR RESEARCH:

- Ask them about their dissertation research.
- Ask them about any new projects that they have undertaken.
- Ask them about any grants they have applied or are in the process of applying for.
- Ask them about what kind of methodologies they use.
- If they do theoretical research, ask them about real-world applications.
- Ask them about their data—whether they collect it themselves, or if are they using secondary data.
- Ask them which journals they are expected to publish in.
- Ask them about any projects they've laid aside and why.

While the best way to learn about faculty research is from the source, it is also important to get an overview of the research of the entire group of faculty in your area. To do that, it's helpful to review their departmental webpages and CVs. There may be some faculty who just list their research in broad strokes (e.g., "Latin American Literature") but it's at least a place to start. We recommend tracking your faculty's research in a more systematic and methodical way and documenting it in a way that can be easily accessed and searched. Using citation management software can be an effective way to do so.[3] A few years ago when our library transitioned to an engaged liaison model, I (Ellen) undertook a project to systematically understand the research in my departments using the Zotero citation management system.[4] I reviewed departmental webpages and CVs and searched through databases to find, download, or enter the publications of each faculty member. The process took a substantial amount of time to complete, but it was invaluable to me, not only in getting to know what each faculty member was researching, but also for gaining knowledge about the broader department's relationship to the library and library resources. For example, I had been puzzled for a while as to why one of my departments had not responded much to my attempts at engagement. In downloading their research publications into my Zotero library I had a realization: the majority of the faculty in the department (which is a professional discipline) were practitioners, not researchers (read more about practitioners in chapter 9). I refocused my engagement efforts on the faculty who had robust research agendas, which brought about invitations to provide library instruction in some upper-level research-focused classes. Over the years, providing quality services to those specific faculty members I focused on has given me a good reputation with the rest of the faculty in the department.

Another great way to learn about your faculty's research interests is to follow them on social media. While this could mean "friending" them on Facebook or following them on Twitter, it also means following them on more academically or professionally focused social networking sites. We have seen our faculty share all kinds of insight into their research via social media, including links to published articles and books, university press releases, blog posts, radio or podcast interviews, and even clips in documentaries. We've even answered research questions from our faculty members over social media!

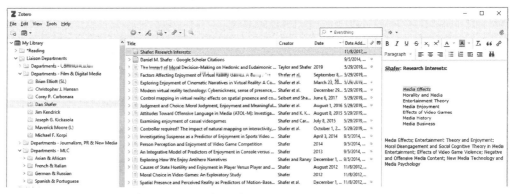

Figure 2.1. Capturing faculty research with Zotero

ACADEMIC OR PROFESSIONAL SOCIAL NETWORKING SITES:

- Academia.edu—"Academia.edu is a platform for academics to share research papers."[5] On Academia.edu, you can follow researchers according to their institutional affiliation or research interests. You can also save publications to your personal library.
- ResearchGate—"ResearchGate is the professional network for scientists and researchers."[6] With Research Gate, you can follow researchers or a project. On your feed you can see when people post new articles and research items or follow a project.
- Google Scholar—"Google Scholar provides a simple way to broadly search for scholarly literature."[7] With Google Scholar, you can follow researchers by name, institution, or research interest; view research impact metrics; and follow profiles to receive alerts about new publications, citations, or related research.
- Mendeley—"Mendeley is a free reference manager and academic social network that can help you organize your research, collaborate with others online, and discover the latest research."[8] With the social network aspect of Mendeley, you can join public or private groups based on research interests and follow specific researchers and read the publications that they have uploaded.
- GitHub—"GitHub is the world's most secure, most scalable, and most loved developer platform."[9] Even though GitHub was originally created as an online host for software code, any academics and researchers who are working on collaborative projects can use GitHub as an easy way to track changes and versions. It provides an easy way to follow other users and projects of interest.
- LinkedIn—LinkedIn is "the world's largest professional network."[10] With LinkedIn, you can connect to people and see their professional profile, which includes expertise and skills. LinkedIn users can also post and share links to their feed.

⊚ Getting to Know Their Teaching

A second important area to get to know about your departments is the curriculum. Which faculty members normally teach which classes? What new topics are being offered in upper-level seminar classes? What are the required classes for each major or program? Which classes are research or writing intensive? Is there a specific research methods class for the discipline? Is there a senior-level capstone class that requires a major project or paper? Which classes are being offered online as well as in person?

These are all good questions to ask as you start to get to know the flow of teaching in your department. Some of these questions can be answered by looking through the course catalog where you can find the requirements for the major and the listing or schedule of courses for each semester, which will tell you who is teaching which class. Other questions may need to be answered by an undergraduate program director or other faculty member. If your campus has an easy way to view syllabi through a learning management system, downloading and reading through them will help you figure out which classes will be research and writing intensive. It will also help you discover if there are resources that the library needs to purchase to meet the instructional requirements.

⊚ Getting to Know Their Broader Contexts

Departmental faculty do not live in a vacuum. Departments are part of a larger context of a school or college and often their futures depend on that larger institutional framework. It is entirely possible that your specific liaison assignment is to a whole school or college, in which case, learning about the broader context is essential. Examine the school's or college's website and see if there is a mission or vision statement or strategic plan. It is important to know if the school or college is planning on doubling the number of majors in a specific department, or adding faculty in a particular research concentration, or cutting departments because of shrinking budgets.

> If your liaison assignment is to a school or college, add the dean, any associate deans, or dean's office staff to your list of people to get to know.

Another good way to understand the broader context of your liaison areas is serving on any related campus committees if you are able. Campus committees are places where university business and policies are worked on and they can give you a bird's eye view of strategic directions that the institution is headed in and where your liaison areas (and of course the library itself) fit into those plans. If the librarians at your institution are permitted to serve on these committees, they can be very strategic. Some committees to consider include:

- curriculum committee
- general education committee
- research committees (policy, human subjects, animal care and use, institutional research board, undergraduate research)
- teaching committees (awards, teaching with technology)

- disciplinary advisory committees (prehealth, prelaw)
- campus diversity committee
- academic freedom committee
- faculty or staff council (depending on your status as a librarian)
- search committees for faculty in your departments, academic deans, or other administrators

GETTING TO KNOW STUDENTS

We have not emphasized getting to know students in any systematized way, mainly because they are only around for a few years before they graduate, unlike the more permanent faculty and staff. Building relationships with faculty and engaging with them in their teaching gives you access to engage with students in the most structured way. However, there are a few other ways we recommend getting to know students that have proven helpful:

- Audit classes, especially ones that are required for the majors in your liaison areas.
- Attend student academic organization meetings related to your liaison areas (e.g., Neuroscience Student Organization or the Public Relations Student Society).
- Attend student affinity group organization meetings in your liaison area (e.g., the Society of Women Engineers, or the Latinx Prehealth Student Association).
- Attend student major information sessions or social hours.

When considering attending student functions, please make sure to secure permission to attend from departmental authorities and student organization leaders.

Be creative—you never know when engagement with students will open doors with the faculty.

To read a story of how one liaison got to know undergraduate students through auditing classes, see the story by Garrett Trott.

Getting a New Liaison Assignment When You Don't Know the Discipline

Perhaps you are a librarian new to the profession and have accepted a job as a liaison librarian. Maybe you majored in English literature as an undergraduate, and now find yourself as a liaison to political science. Or you majored in psychology and now have been assigned a Health Science department. Or consider the scenario in which another liaison librarian in your department retires, and their departments need to be served on an interim basis until a new librarian can be hired. How do you gain an understanding of a new field of study so as to effectively serve the students and faculty in your liaison areas?

The first thing to remember is your training as a librarian—you can do the research! Think about the ways that you would help a student gain knowledge in an unfamiliar area of study: get background knowledge from references sources, locate important articles and books in the field, and read review articles to get a good overview of the state of research in niche areas.

Sign up for table of contents alerts for major journals in the field to see what kinds of research topics are being published. Search through the library literature using the academic subject as a keyword to find articles that discuss the information-seeking behavior of students and faculty in the discipline, the major issues in collection development, the way other librarians have provided information literacy instruction. Sign up for a professional librarian listserv devoted to your discipline (if one exists). Attend lectures in the department; ones aimed at undergraduates will often paint a picture of the discipline that can be helpful for you as you seek to understand it. Look at the resources page of the disciplinary association—look at their "about" page or their strategic plan (if they have one), and definitely look at their "resources" page, which is a wealth of information about teaching and research in those areas. And of course don't forget to ask! As we have already said previously, talk to the faculty about their research and teaching—it will help you to start to understand the discipline as a whole as well.

◎ Story of Getting to Know a Community

Stories can be read in the supplement at the publisher's website.
www.liaisonengagementsuccess.com

- Opening Doors for Engagement with Students—by Garrett Trott, Corban University
  "I was amazed at how much I learned through a course on Classical Hebrew. I took this course expecting to learn the language: syntax, grammar, vocabulary, etc. Because I could not help but look at it through the eyes of a librarian, I learned so much more through this course by intentionally looking for ways to better serve students and faculty."

◎ Key Points

- Your liaison areas are made up of a community of people whom you should make it your first priority to get to know.
- Developing relationships with key people in your liaison areas will help you expand your network.
- The people in your liaison areas are busy with research and teaching, and it is important to understand their interests and practices in these areas.
- If you are systematic in the way that you interact with your liaison areas, it will help you engage more meaningfully with them.

⊚ Notes

1. José O. Díaz and Meris A. Mandernach, "Relationship Building One Step at a Time: Case Studies of Successful Faculty-Librarian Partnerships," *Portal: Libraries and the Academy* 17, no. 2 (April 8, 2017): 273–82, https://doi.org/10.1353/pla.2017.0016.

2. John G. Bales, "Making All the Right Moves for Liaison Engagement: A Strategy for Relating to Faculty," *College and Research Libraries News* 76, no. 10 (2015): 551, https://doi.org/10.5860/crln.76.10.9400.

3. Ellen Hampton Filgo, "Systematically Understanding Faculty Needs: Using Zotero in Liaison Work," *College and Research Libraries News* 77, no. 1 (January 1, 2016): 18–22; Scott Marsalis and Julia A. Kelly, "Building a RefWorks Database of Faculty Publications as a Liaison and Collection Development Tool," *Issues in Science and Technology Librarianship* (Summer 2004), http://conservancy.umn.edu/handle/11299/42227.

4. Filgo, "Systematically Understanding Faculty Needs."

5. Academia.edu, "Academia.Edu—About," accessed February 8, 2020, https://www.academia.edu/about.

6. ResearchGate.com, "ResearchGate—About," accessed February 8, 2020, https://www.researchgate.net/about.

7. Google Scholar, "About Google Scholar," accessed February 8, 2020, https://scholar.google.com/intl/en/scholar/about.html.

8. Elsevier Solutions, "Mendeley Database," accessed February 8, 2020, https://www.elsevier.com/solutions/mendeley.

9. GitHub.com, "GitHub," accessed February 8, 2020, https://github.com.

10. LinkedIn.com, "About LinkedIn," accessed February 8, 2020, https://about.linkedin.com/.

Mindsets for Liaison Work

THE FIRST STEP IN DEVELOPING STRATEGIES for liaison work is to consider ways of thinking and ways of being among people that will help set the stage for successful outreach experiences. We will then explore a set of skills and traits that can help you become an outstanding liaison. Whether the things discussed in this chapter are already among your skills or something that will require intentional work for you, it's important to spend time thinking about each of these and identify strengths, areas for growth, blind spots, and challenges.

Mindsets

Mindsets are the unique lenses through which we interpret and navigate life. They are constructed and influenced by many things, including our personality, our upbringing, our environment, and our circumstances. Mindsets often drive the way we behave in a certain situation or the way we create sense making. Stanford psychologist Carol Dweck popularized the idea in her book *Mindset: The New Psychology of Success*, in which she identified two major contrasting viewpoints: fixed mindset and growth mindset.[1] In a fixed mindset, we believe our abilities are innate and cannot evolve over time. The abilities we start with are what we have to work with throughout our life. By contrast, a growth mindset assumes that we can improve our abilities and change with experience, practice, and time. In the former, failure is judgment. In the latter, failure is an opportunity to experiment and improve. Dweck writes,

> People with a fixed mindset are out to prove themselves, and may get very defensive when someone suggests they made a mistake—in other words, they measure themselves by their failures. People with a growth mindset, on the other hand, often show perseverance and resilience when they've committed errors—they become more motivated to work harder.[2]

Whether you are in the growth mindset or fixed mindset camp, it influences how you view yourself, others, and the experiences you share—in this case, particularly the experiences you have when engaging your liaison areas. Are you eager to learn from others or afraid that your interactions might shed light on your gaps or lack of experience or failures? What other mindsets color your view of the world and what effect do they have on your outreach experiences? Is your mindset one of proactivity? Or do you react only when others reach out to you? Is your mindset one of curiosity? Are you always interested in new information that might be useful to your clients and exploring what their research and teaching interests are? Or are you content to investigate only what is asked of you? Is your mindset one of abundance? Do you feel there are plenty of resources and successes to share? Or do you worry there isn't enough (time, opportunities, successes) to go around?[3] For example, if you find yourself thinking "I wish I were more proactive, but I'm reserved, or I worry that I will be bothering others," consider how each of these mindsets might relate to your liaison work and whether they will stand in your way or help you succeed.

◉ Adaptability

Descriptors like *flexible* and *adaptable* might seem like something tied more to personality (think laid back, easy going individual versus laser-focused overachiever), but the truth is, these are attributes you can work on and develop. Often, we think of these terms as being interchangeable, but they have some notable nuanced differences as we think about them in the context of librarian engagement. The term *flexibility* is frequently used with tangible things that can be flexed (like your back or your schedule), but I really like *Merriam-Webster's* third definition as that which is "characterized by a ready capability to adapt to new, different, or changing requirements."[4] We would love to see this line appear at the top of every library job ad. Not only does this definition reflect the changing landscape of modern library work, but it also shines light on the path to successful liaison work. Another important concept in this arena is agility. When we are agile, we are "marked by ready ability to move with quick easy grace."[5] Now maybe you're picturing a dancer rather than a librarian, but this readiness and willingness to pivot gracefully is the true litmus test of excellent liaison librarians as they engage with their constituents. We all know that the world (and the library) won't stand still. The ability to quickly adapt and grow in new ways is the only way to meet the evolving needs of our users. A good example of pivoting is seen in Erin Ware's story, "Pivoting Your Strategy When Pandemics or Other Unexpected Twists Come Your Way" in chapter 4, "Strategies for Outreach."

⑥ Emotional Intelligence

The *Oxford Dictionary of Psychology* defines *emotional intelligence* as the "ability to monitor one's own and other people's emotions, to discriminate between different emotions and label them appropriately, and to use emotional information to guide thinking and behaviour."[6] The term appeared in psychological literature of the late mid to late twentieth century and was widely popularized by science journalist Daniel Goleman in his 1995 book *Emotional Intelligence*. Psychologists Peter Salovey and John D. Mayer formally defined the concept in 1990 to include four component parts.[7] Of these components, the two most directly relevant to effective interpersonal communication include:

- The ability to perceive, appraise, and express emotions
- The ability to comprehend emotional messages and to make use of emotional information

The definition of *emotional intelligence* from *The Oxford Dictionary of Organizational Behavior* captures nicely the connection to the work at hand: it is "the measure of an individual's awareness of and capacity to manage their emotions and the emotions of others through effective relationship management."[8] Emotional intelligence is all about making sense of one's environments and interactions with others. This ability to assess the situation and to respond in meaningful ways that reflect that understanding are crucially important skills for liaisons. This intelligence is central to relationship management, a core issue for successful liaison work. What follows are several important aspects related to emotional intelligence.

⑥ Soft Skills Are . . . Well, "Hard"!

Soft skills might best be considered a loose federation of abilities and traits that center on our interactions and communication with others. Together they make up our ability to interact effectively with others. They are often seen in contrast to hard skills, those that are technical or professional, but soft skills are often much harder to quantify and to master. In fact, these skills can make or break your career. Sometimes we're quick to put soft skills like empathy in the "born with it" category, that is to say, something we either have or we don't, like brown eyes or blue eyes. The truth is that developing soft skills is something anyone can cultivate and there are many great resources for doing so.[9]

Many employers—even libraries—won't care if you have hard skills if you don't also have the soft variety. Peggy Klaus, in her book *The Hard Truth about Soft Skills: Workplace Lessons Smart People Wish They'd Learned Sooner*, says that "mastering soft skills takes persistence. It requires that you be mindful about yourself and your career. Mastering these practical and tactical skills doesn't magically happen overnight. It requires hard work, but the payoff can be tremendous."[10] You might think that soft skills are a recent interest in the workplace, but their significance shows up in the literature from over one hundred years ago.[11] What follows is by no means an exhaustive list of soft skills, but highlights several that are important to being an engaged librarian.

⑥ Empathy

Empathy may not show up at the top of the list on that library job ad, but it can play a significant role in your ability to connect successfully to the clients you serve. This ability to put yourself in someone else's shoes, or understand their experience from their point of view, is foundational to building connection with others, and its importance has been noted in many fields where communication and connection are important between practitioner and constituent.[12]

Empathy requires us to slow down, to pay attention, and to listen. It means focusing on the other person and their experiences, rather than our own agenda, and that's a lot harder than it sounds. Often, we get caught in the trap of thinking about the end goal over the moment at hand. Have you ever been thinking about how that conversation with a faculty member will benefit you? Will this conversation lead to an important instruction session or count as a research consultation on your annual review? Roman Krznaric, author of *Empathy: Why It Matters, and How to Get It*, says that the "real competitive advantage of the human worker will be their capacity to create relationships, which means empathy will count more than experience."[13] Without empathy, you can't build strong relationships, and without relationships, we would argue that you cannot be a successful liaison librarian.

⑥ Listening

While it might seem like a passive activity, listening is hard work! Genuine listening is a powerful and positive tool for engaging with another person, but it's a discipline that requires practice and intention. What's much easier than listening well? Failing to do so. There are many reasons people fail to listen. Sometimes we're in too big of a hurry, or too busy figuring out the next thing we want to say. Sometimes we're too focused on our own agenda or just uncomfortable with the possibility of silence in the conversation. Sometimes it's because of assumptions we're holding, about the person we're talking to, or what they think, or what we intended to get out of the conversation. When we listen actively, we are paying attention to what's being said without rushing to judgment or assuming we already know what the other person is trying to say. It includes reflecting on what we're hearing by asking for clarification of the things we're hearing and summarizing what we've heard, both to make sure we're understanding and to communicate that back to the other person.[14]

Listening requires us to step outside ourselves, to quiet our own noise, and to take the spotlight off of ourselves.[15] There are many ways to practice the art of listening, including inviting input, affirming that another's thoughts are important, observing body language, allowing silence and space, making eye contact, removing other distractions, and taking notes, to name just a few. Even when we know what to do, it can still be hard. Creating more space for conversation as well as creating time for reflection are important, even when it seems impossible.

DOS AND DON'TS OF LISTENING
(ADAPTED FROM PEGGY KLAUS)[16]

- Be present and focused.
- Remove other distractions.
- Quiet your own internal noise.
- Keep an open mind.
- Listen attentively.
- Pay attention to nonverbal cues (body language, gesture, tone, etc.).
- Pay attention to your own nonverbal signals.
- Withhold judgment.
- Ask questions to clarify understanding.
- Don't be in a hurry.
- Don't assume or judge.
- Don't multitask or let your mind wander.
- Don't interrupt with your thoughts or advice.
- Don't assume you're being asked to solve a problem.
- Don't figure out what you want to say next while the other person is talking.
- Don't be afraid of silence in the conversation.
- Don't take the conversation off into a different direction.

SIX WAYS TO BECOME A BETTER LISTENER
ACCORDING TO STEPHANIE VOZZA[17]

- Listen to learn, not to be polite.
- Quiet your agenda.
- Ask more questions.
- Pay attention to your talk/listen ratio.
- Repeat back what you heard.
- Wait until someone is done talking before you respond.

⟲ Relationship Building

It's important to frame all of the skills and traits discussed here as abilities that enhance relationship building. Imagine a carpenter whose only tool was a screwdriver or a doctor whose only tool was a stethoscope. You don't want to be that kind of professional. When we are focused on fostering these relationships, we are balancing the needs of others with our own. We don't approach our work with the "reference desk" model, where we sit passively waiting for others to come to us, but rather make ourselves available proactively. This often includes not only a mindset of openness and availability, but a geographic availability as well. By that, we mean being in the spaces where your constituents are, not expecting them to always come to you in your own space. This approach might take the form of officing in the department; it might mean regular visits to the department or being visible at departmental events.

As you think about the many different kinds of relationships you have, professionally and personally, remember that they are all different. There's not just one way to relate to others, and that holds true in your work as a liaison too. Different people respond to different approaches and need different things. If you ever hear a liaison librarian tell you, "This is the only way you should do it," you should be skeptical of their approach.

Figure 3.1. Business Liaison Librarian Carol Schuetz holding office hours at the Baylor Hankamer School of Business. *Photo credit: Eric Ames*

Communication

While we often think of *communication* as an umbrella term for the various mediums through which we communicate (email, phone, chat, text, in person), it's important to remember that everything under this umbrella is intricately tied to interpersonal skills. Regardless of the communication medium or tool, it's important to always consider how interpersonal skills influence and affect your communication. You should be considerate and respectful of other people's time and attention. Your particular work culture will certainly influence and nuance this, but remember that the workplace is a delicate balance of productive work and collegiality.

Be intentional about the medium of communication. Before communicating, actively consider the following:

- Need—who needs the information and who needs to respond to the information?
- Importance—what is the importance or urgency of the information?
- Method—what's the best communication tool for this particular situation?

Who needs to know? Is this information part of a private conversation? Is it meant for a group? Do you need colleagues in your department to weigh in on something? This is particularly challenging with email, because it's easy to think "more is better" and add too many people to your email. There are, of course, times where the information you're sending needs to go to your whole liaison department, but there are also times when the information might be better focused to a smaller, relevant audience. "I know only a few people are knowledgeable about this topic or need to know this information, but isn't it easier to just send it to the whole department?" said the person who just annoyed every recipient of the email. Of course, sometimes it can be hard to tell who can answer your question or who needs the information you have to share. Do you communicate separately with each person? Do you keep them all together in an email? This certainly depends on the nature of the information. Sometimes you get caught up in thinking, "I'm not exactly sure who all needs this" or "better safe than sorry," so you send the email to many people. Different people will feel differently about this. Some people want to know everything there is to know (and want you to feel the same way) and some feel like they are constantly trying to keep ahead of their inbox. In the end, it's important to consider the recipient's communication preferences and, when possible, their state of mind at the time. We realize this is a lot to consider when you're just trying to get a message communicated, but it may be important to think about whether you want the receiver to be focused or distracted, whether you need to talk with them or just to send information.

Consider that the different modes of communication function in different ways and demand (or don't demand) different things of other people. Be thoughtful about the modes and which one might best suit the situation. Consider if it is a time-sensitive issue. Consider the other person's schedule and commitments. Consider the other person's communication preferences. If someone drops by your workspace and you're there, they have forced you into this mode of communication (but see recommendations in the next paragraph for how to handle this). If someone emails you, you can choose to respond when you have time or are prepared to answer; maybe you need to gather some information before responding. Is the information time sensitive or something you'll need to archive for later use? Sometimes a tool like Slack or Microsoft Teams can be a better solution for more ephemeral communication, but this will depend on your institutional culture.

One of the beauties and burdens of in-person communication is that you have a livestream of verbal and nonverbal cues. If you're stopping by, especially unannounced, make sure you are reading cues about openness, availability, and busyness. Some people are better than others at reading these cues, but we should all be aware that these cues exist, whether or not the other person you're with is consciously aware of them. Remember that just because something is important or urgent to you at this moment, it may not have the same priority for the other person. Be careful not to drop in every time you have a question. Consider whether or not you need an answer immediately. Can it wait? Can you send your question another way (via email or chat)? Is your question going to require something of the recipient before they can answer? Can you save your question for a meeting you already have scheduled? Is this something you can table until a better time for the person answering your question? In an unexpected interaction like a surprise drop in, make sure to give the other person an out. You can do this by asking questions like:

- "Do you have time for a quick question?"
- "Do you have two minutes for me?"

- "Is now a good time? If not, I can come back later."
- "Do you have time this week to discuss X?"
- "Can I send you a meeting invitation to discuss X?"

While all of the soft skills are important, communication is one that is fraught with so many potential pitfalls and consequences. Thoughtful and intentional communication can positively affect your liaison relationships. If you don't pay attention to the ways in which you communicate or don't read the cues from those you're communicating with, your liaison work will definitely suffer. In summary, Peggy Klaus notes that one thing is certain: "[W]hether you are addressing one or one thousand people—face-to-face, on the phone, or through the wires—your communication skills or lack thereof, can make or break your career."[18] Tread carefully and thoughtfully, because you never know how your communication can positively or negatively affect the relationships on which your work as a liaison depends.

None of the concepts discussed in this chapter is exclusive to the domain of liaison work, but we can't stress enough how important they are to successful relationships and therefore to successful liaison work. A lack of awareness and lack of active cultivation of these crucial mindsets can create insurmountable obstacles to the work of a liaison, but devoting energy to them can establish a strong foundation for liaison work. Emotional intelligence and related soft skills such as adaptability, empathy, and active listening require the challenging work of mindfulness and reflection. We strongly encourage individual liaisons and liaison programs to make space for professional and personal development in these areas, signaling the importance of these skills and ways of thinking.

Key Points

- Crucial building blocks to successful liaison work include a growth mindset, adaptability, emotional intelligence, and soft skills.
- While these skills may be easier for some and more difficult for others, it is possible to intentionally cultivate these areas.
- Relationship building is the cornerstone to all liaison work.

Notes

1. Carol S. Dweck, *Mindset: The New Psychology of Success*, illustrated edition (New York: Random House, 2006).

2. Gary Klein, "Mindsets: What They Are and Why They Matter," *Psychology Today*, May 1, 2016, https://www.psychologytoday.com/blog/seeing-what-others-dont/201605/mindsets.

3. The term "abundance mentality or mindset" was coined in Stephen R. Covey, *The 7 Habits of Highly Effective People* (New York: Simon and Schuster Sound Ideas, 1989).

4. Merriam-Webster, "Flexible," accessed October 24, 2020, https://www.merriam-webster.com/dictionary/flexible.

5. Merriam-Webster, "Agile," accessed October 24, 2020, https://www.merriam-webster.com/dictionary/agile.

6. Andrew M. Colman, ed., "Emotional Intelligence," in *A Dictionary of Psychology*, Oxford Reference Online (Oxford: University Press, 2015).

7. Colman.

8. Emma Jeanes, ed., "Emotional Intelligence," in *A Dictionary of Organizational Behaviour* (Oxford University Press, January 24, 2019), https://www.oxfordreference.com/view/10.1093/acref/9780191843273.001.0001/acref-9780191843273.

9. "Empathy: How Do I Cultivate It?" *Greater Good*, accessed October 24, 2020, https://greatergood.berkeley.edu/topic/empathy/definition.

10. Peggy Klaus, *The Hard Truth about Soft Skills: Workplace Lessons Smart People Wish They'd Learned Sooner*, 1st ed. (New York: HarperCollins, 2007).

11. A 1916 study in *Engineering Education* reported 1,500 engineers replying to the survey question: "What are the most important factors in determining probable success or failure in engineering? mentioned personal qualities more than seven times as frequently as they did knowledge of engineering science and technique of practice." Charles Riborg Mann, *A Study of Engineering Education: Prepared for the Joint Committee on Engineering Education of the National Engineering Societies* (Massachusetts: Merrymount Press, 1918), 106, https://hdl.handle.net/2027/wu.89077496529.

12. P. S. Bellet and M. J. Maloney, "The Importance of Empathy as an Interviewing Skill in Medicine," *JAMA: The Journal of the American Medical Association* 266, no. 13 (1991): 1831–32, https://doi.org/10.1001/jama.266.13.1831.

13. Roman Krznaric, personal communication with author, June 26, 2020.

14. Center for Creative Leadership, "Use Active Listening Skills When Coaching Others," accessed October 24, 2020, https://www.ccl.org/articles/leading-effectively-articles/coaching-others-use-active-listening-skills/.

15. Sha Towers, "Listening as Leadership," *Baylor University Human Resources: Learn and Lead*, n.d.

16. Klaus, *The Hard Truth about Soft Skills*, 55.

17. Stephanie Vozza, "6 Ways to Become a Better Listener," *Fast Company*, March 17, 2017, https://www.fastcompany.com/3068959/6-ways-to-become-a-better-listener.

18. Klaus, *The Hard Truth about Soft Skills*, 52.

Strategies for Outreach

THIS CHAPTER EXPLORES SPECIFIC THINGS you can do to expand the reach of your liaison work and make the kinds of connections with constituents that will allow you to succeed. Here you'll find some specific suggestions of methods and strategies for communicating and networking. Remember, there's no one right way to do this and some strategies will be more successful in certain situations or seasons. Our recommendation is to add as many of these as you can to your list of possibilities to draw on as you decide which strategy works best for the specific job.

⊚ Email and Newsletters

Emailing your constituents is an efficient way to communicate information and the services you and your library offer. This approach can provide you with a good way to organize and economize what you want to tell them about yourself and the variety of ways you can help the faculty and students you serve. For many faculty members, having this kind of information documented where they can refer back to it at the point of need is especially useful. Some liaison librarians compile newsletter-type information directly in a nicely formatted email. Others compose a newsletter that can be physically distributed or placed on departmental bulletin boards, although these can be distributed via email as well.

Letters from your Librarian
School of Education
SPRING 2020

WELCOME NOTE

Hello! My name is Amy James and I am the Director of Instruction and Information Literacy/Interim Director of Public Services here at the Central Libraries. I am also the library liaison to the School of Education. That means that I have the opportunity to partner with you to help your students reach their academic goals when it comes to information literacy and the research process. I am looking forward to working with you and your students this spring semester, 2020. Below is a list of some updates and ways that we can work together this upcoming semester. If we haven't met yet, please send me an email. I'd love to meet and buy you a coffee!

WAYS TO PARTNER WITH A LIBRARIAN

The library's website now contains a link to our information literacy instruction services (baylor.edu/lib under the "services" tab). In addition to ways that you can partner with a librarian, you'll also find out more about our information literacy mission, goals, materials (including ready-made learning modules on various information literacy related topics), and statistics.
https://researchguides.baylor.edu/infoliteracy/partner

RESEARCH GUIDES

Would a custom course guide benefit your students? Reach out to me and we can design a research guide with information specific and relevant to your students that they can access at any time. See examples under the education subheading at: researchguides.baylor.edu.

CONTACT INFORMATION
AMY JAMES
EMAIL:
AMY_B_JAMES@BAYLOR.EDU
OFFICE: 254-710-2335

INFORMATION LITERACY INSTRUCTION

Interested in having your students come into the library for a session on research basics, evaluating information, conducting a literature review, etc.? Contact me using the form at: https://researchguides.baylor.edu/infoliteracy/schedule and we will work together to build a class session that will benefit your students. Sessions are available online and in person.

BOOK & ARTICLE REQUESTS

If there is an item that you'd like to gain access to and you don't see it listed on our website, please feel free to contact me at amy_b_james@baylor.edu and I will do my best to request it through interlibrary loan or purchase it for our collection.

Figure 4.1. Liaison email newsletter to departmental faculty. *Photo credit: Amy James*

Depending on the relationships you have with the faculty or the particular culture of the department, you may have an administrative associate or a department chair forward your information or you may set up an email group to contact the intended audience directly. It would be a good idea to discuss this with the departmental stakeholders to determine the best method. You may have completely different approaches depending on the cultural climate of each department you serve. Another consideration is the frequency and timing of this type of communication. Be careful about overloading your recipients by sending updates too frequently. Of course, this depends on your particular relationships, but overdoing it can wear out your welcome and have a negative effect on your work. Keep in mind that people respond to mass mailings and group emails in different ways, too. Some people ignore messages sent to a large group, maybe assuming if it's really important, one of the other recipients will let them know or just deciding that it's not something they personally need to respond to or act on because it went to many people. We've heard of people who only respond to emails from their boss, which you may consider irresponsible, but if that's the case, you don't need to take it personally. The main thing is to make sure you know your audience. We've sent departmental messages to which we received no replies until we saw recipients in person. In person, they seemed enthusiastic about the information or wanted to follow up on it with us. In the end, for messages you send to a group or in bulk, don't assume that just because you sent it that everyone read it, processed it, or filed it away for safekeeping. With this in mind, this kind of communication approach may be best in tandem with other strategies.

⊚ Personal Meetings

As with any strategy for interaction, there are pros and cons to personal meetings. They can be time consuming and less scalable than mass communication, but positively, they can be customized to the individual and are an even stronger way to build relationships. This also allows you to be more adaptive in the course of the conversation. Maybe you intended to talk with a faculty member about a new service the library is offering, but in the course of the conversation, you realize from what they've shared with you that this service isn't as directly applicable as you first thought and that they're much more interested in something else you weren't thinking would be of use to them. Based on what you learn from the conversation about the individual's needs and interests, you can pivot the conversation to focus more on what is immediately useful or interesting to them.

Remember to be mindful of faculty time and commitments. You may enjoy chatting with them for hours (and maybe the feeling is mutual) but both of you probably have other commitments. Watch for verbal and nonverbal cues that indicate they've had enough or have somewhere else to be. Make sure you're not inadvertently making them feel trapped, because that never has a positive outcome on your outreach.

When possible, set up a meeting that's convenient for them, whether it's at their office or building or at a time or day that works best for them. If your institutional culture works this way, send a calendar invitation so they not only have a reminder, but a sense of how long a conversation to expect. We recommend that you set up the meeting in the library only if there is a clear advantage for them to come to you, not you to them. Examples of this might be that you need to evaluate an instruction space you'll be using with their class or showing them something that can't leave the building like spaces for faculty or special collections that might enhance their teaching. If you're fortunate enough to have a coffee shop or café in your library, this can be a draw—especially when paired with you offering to buy drinks. Even though our library has a coffee shop, we've occasionally brought coffee to faculty members when meeting in their office across campus.

Another good way to build relationships and positively influence engagement is by participating in events on your campus that aren't about you "doing library outreach." This is more about presence in the larger community and might include things like serving on campus committees together, attending or volunteering for commencement ceremonies, or helping with campus move-in days. Encounters like this outside of normal habitats remind us of the way young children will often assume that their teacher lives at the school, because that's the only place they've encountered their teacher, and it's only when they run into their teacher at the grocery store or somewhere else in the world—and are shocked to see them there—that they realize teachers are more multidimensional than they had realized. In that same way, serving on committees together or attending campus events reminds your faculty and students that you too are multidimensional and these encounters keep you on their radar.

One particular type of campus connection that's important to consider is the one specific to the interests of the faculty member or department you're serving. Often these are events sponsored by the department, like lectures, performances, colloquia, showcases, and exhibitions. Don't overlook adjacent events such as ones that are not department or campus sponsored but that nonetheless are important to your faculty and students. In the prepandemic days, I (Sha) attended an off-campus art gallery opening reception knowing that one of my art faculty members was exhibiting in the show. I attended another event where a faculty member's local jazz combo was performing, just to show support and interest in what was important to that colleague. This geographic proximity is where the magic begins. We can't tell you how many times we've encountered faculty members at events such as these who say things like, "Oh, I'm so glad to see you, because I've been meaning to talk to you about working with my class" or "When can I come visit with you about my research?" These are questions they could easily have emailed or called about but crossing paths in person is what made it happen.

⊚ Serendipitous Encounters

Some of our favorite encounters are the serendipitous ones—the ones you can't plan for, don't expect, and just surprise you. They happen when you're not even thinking about your job or the departments with which you work. They occur at the grocery store, the gym, the local bookstore, while dropping off kids at school, or in line at a coffee shop. To be fair, these kinds of connections rarely happen on their own; there is often some background work or connection that makes it possible. Perhaps you've built a relationship with the person already, or maybe you recently sent them a new faculty welcome email, or maybe a friend or colleague just introduced you. We've built up a lot of credibility with students and faculty while waiting in line at our library's Starbucks. Part of it, we're sure, is the shared experience of needing coffee. There's also probably a little of the multidimensionality aspect mentioned earlier because it's nice just to see librarians as normal humans. Encounters like these are also nonthreatening; you're not out canvasing the academic neighborhood passing out flyers or showing up at a faculty member's office like those door-to-door salespeople you want to avoid. One particular flavor of the serendipitous encounter that's been really fruitful for me is when I (Sha) am going to an appointment with a faculty member or delivering something to them and I run into another faculty member. Without exception they're glad to see me and visit briefly. And something else I've noticed is that colleagues get drawn in when they see me talking to someone else in the department and want to be part of whatever's going on. You might be asking, "Wouldn't it be easier and faster just to send things through campus mail or send off a quick email?" Yes, it would, but here's the important trade off: we believe a significant part of why these encounters are successful is because the faculty members are seeing you where they work—on their turf—taking time out of your daily routine to be among them. It communicates that you care about them and are invested in them. It signals to them that you are part of their community. You might be asking yourself, "How can unplanned encounters be a strategy? How do you plan for that?" While you can't force this type of liaison engagement, you can position yourself well for this by geography and openness. If you only work in your office, you'll see less of this kind of encounter. When and where it makes sense, put yourself in the geographic landscape of the people you're serving, whether that's in public spaces on campus or in the buildings or spaces of the departments you serve. The other significant piece of laying the foundation for this kind of encounter is a mindfulness and openness to unexpected encounters. If you're looking for some tips on how to make these encounters fail, we have a few. If you always act harried, that will do it. If you're always on your phone, that's a negative signal as well. However, if you allow yourself to be open and aware, if you take in the world around you with an air of friendliness, these connections will happen with little or no effort.

Personal Connections and Building Relationships

Regardless of the mechanism or strategy you use in your liaison engagement with faculty and students, the development of personal connections and the building of relationships lays the foundation for success. Use every opportunity you have to get to know the people you're serving. One example of how you might do this is to pay attention to announcements of new faculty joining your institution. Learn about the person—where they've come from, what their professional interests are, what areas will they be teaching or researching in. Send them a welcome email and invite them to an informal time, such as coffee or lunch, to get to know them. Of course, these encounters are for you to discover their needs and how you can support them, but don't rush to make this transactional. Enjoy getting to know them. To continue building relationships, keep an eye out for news of recent accomplishments, new books released, leadership appointments in a professional society, and article publications by the faculty you're working with. Getting to know them on a personal level, however, demands tact on your part. You have to really pay close attention to subtle cues. Doing so can strengthen a relationship and not doing it can put people off. The culture of your workplace and the department with which you are working may signal the openness or closure to this type of connection, and you'll have to work really hard to determine what's appropriate, expected, or frowned upon for any given situation. Maybe asking someone about their personal interests, hobbies, pets, or kids will be a welcome connection point or it could be met with icy discomfort. This arena will rely heavily on social and emotional insight. During a meeting that I (Sha) had with a faculty member, we talked about our kids, spouses, and our dogs, and these shared experiences have positively affected how we've worked together in designing classes. However, not every faculty member wants to know about your personal life or wants you to know about theirs.

- Departmental lectures
- Committee work
- Clinical rounds
- Faculty book interviews
- Award ceremonies
- Student groups
- Pop-up library
- Social media
- Liaison listed on departmental website
- Attending concerts, lectures, presentations
- Serving on thesis committees
- Lunch, coffee, or drinks

Identifying Key Stakeholders

All of the topics discussed so far in this chapter are, in some way, about networking, whether it's strategically planned or the result of openness to situations and opportunities around you. There is one more aspect of networking we'd like to mention here: identifying key stakeholders. Such identification is doing your homework and leveraging connections to bring key stakeholders into your orbit. This was discussed briefly in chapter 2, but as a reminder, part of your successful work is figuring out who these people are. Maybe they are the obvious ones like division or department chairs. Maybe they are invisible movers and shakers like administrative assistants, or a beloved, longtime faculty member in the department. Often, being able to identify these people will maximize your influence and scale your time and energy. For example, if you build a good relationship with an administrative assistant, chair, or dean, and your communication to faculty members routes through them, it might be more effective than a bunch of individual contacts. This example touches on another important aspect of identifying key stakeholders, and we like to call this the power of "network triangulation." Sometimes your success or power comes from "who you know." What we mean is that your connection with a well-respected person signals to others that they can trust you or that you have significance. Imagine if you saw a colleague of yours having coffee with the president of the university or the dean of a school; you might think, "I didn't know she had that person's ear!" or "He has more connections than I thought." When students that you serve see their professor connecting well with you, it signals to them that you are a trustworthy or knowledgeable. If junior faculty members see you positively interacting with senior faculty in their department or their chair or dean, then they begin to realize you are someone they should connect with. If you put yourself in the role of a person observing this network triangulation scenario, you might say to yourself, "If I trust person A and person A trusts you, then I can trust you, too." While this works well in passive observation settings like those described here, it also works in more active settings, in which a person of influence introduces you to their students or their colleagues. This can accelerate liaison networking success, whereas

To learn about having to change an outreach strategy unexpectedly, see the story by Erin Ware. To understand how a change in strategy can bring about success with instruction, see the story by Jennifer L. A. Whelan.

on your own, without the introductions, you will have to invest much more time building the relationship and proving to the person that you're trustworthy or someone they should get to know. Leveraging these key stakeholders can also get you access to other venues and audiences. For example, saying to a new junior faculty, "It sure would be nice if I got invited to attend one of your faculty meetings" is very different than asking an administrative assistant that you've built a good relationship with to put in a good word for you with the chair or dean. Better yet, if you've built a good relationship with the chair or dean—the people who actually decide who gets to attend that meeting or gets on the agenda—you can talk to them directly about your desire to attend or you can offer to come talk to the faculty about new things your library is doing for the faculty and students. If you get invited to attend such a meeting, networking triangulation is on full display. The entire faculty then sees that you are important enough to be invited or to speak or that you are trusted by the decision makers in their department.

Stories of Outreach Strategies

Stories can be read in the supplement at the publisher's website.
www.liaisonengagementsuccess.com

- Pivoting Your Strategy when Pandemics or Other Unexpected Twists Come Your Way—by Erin Ware, Louisiana State University Health, Shreveport
    "While this was not an ideal way to establish a relationship with the doctors and residents who make up that department, it was definitely the best I could do in a difficult situation, and the final product is something I can use in the future whenever new people join the faculty throughout the year."
- Extracurricular Engagement as an Alternative to Traditional Instruction—by Jennifer L. A. Whelan, College of the Holy Cross
    "Participation in the MID [Manuscripts, Inscriptions and Documents Club] has drastically reformed my relationship with the Classics department, increasing my visibility to faculty, enhancing my relationship with students, and generally creating a liaison relationship where I am not an incidental library contact, but a recognized 'member' of the department."

Key Points

- Be intentional, thoughtful, and proactive about communicating with your constituents.
- Being engaged in your campus and departmental communities is beneficial to developing strong liaison connections.

- Be open to the unexpected and unplanned encounters and opportunities.
- Identify the key stakeholders among your liaison assignments.
- Remember that building relationships establishes the potential for successful outreach.

⑥ Note

1. Neil Nero and Anne Langley, "Subject Liaisons in Academic Libraries: An Open Access Data Set from 2015," *Portal: Libraries and the Academy* 17, no. 1 (2017): 5–15, https://doi.org/10.1353/pla.2017.0001.

Engagement with the Humanities

ENGAGING WITH STAKEHOLDERS IN THE HUMANITIES may seem on the surface like an easy task for librarians; after all, 41 percent of librarians come from a humanities disciplinary background at the undergraduate level.[1] However, the experience of attaining an undergraduate humanities degree does not necessarily mean that a librarian understands how researchers in the humanities perceive and use the library and its resources and services. In addition, the humanities have undergone a shift during the last century—the entire subfield of the digital humanities (DH) has come to prominence since the advent of the internet. A liaison librarian assigned to humanities disciplines needs the ability to understand its disciplines and how its researchers and teachers operate to effectively engage with and provide services and resources to their faculty and students.

What Are the Humanities?

The *humanities* have been defined as "the disciplines that investigate the expressions of the human mind," unlike the study of nature or humans in their social context (which belongs to science and social sciences, respectively), and include such things as language, literature, art, music, philosophy, theater, and poetry.[2] Scholars of the humanities collect, teach, criticize, and interpret the products of the human mind. Libraries and library collections have always been a natural friend to the humanities as they are the laboratory domain of the humanist.

TRADITIONAL HUMANITIES DISCIPLINES[3]

- Classics
- History
- Literature
- Philosophy
- Religion
- Performing arts (we will address this in chapter 8)
- Visual arts (we will address this in chapter 8)

OTHER HUMANITIES-RELATED DISCIPLINES

- Anthropology (can also be considered a social science)
- Archaeology (can also be considered a social science)
- Linguistics and languages (can also be considered a social science)
- Law and politics (can also be considered a social science or a profession)

How Do Humanists Research?

According to a recent Ithaka S+R report, humanities researchers:

- Collect large amounts of information in both digital and print format.
- Primarily work independently and have a low interest in collaborative research.
- Use student research assistance.
- Perceive their research skills as advanced.
- Engage with and rely on information professionals, most likely for help finding and accessing primary materials.
- Value librarians as teaching and learning partners.[4]

In addition to the report from Ithaka S+R, the Modern Language Association (MLA) has explored how humanists research. At the 2020 MLA conference, a roundtable was held to discuss "recent advances and obstacles in the production, dissemination, and institutional evaluation of [humanities] research."[5] The broad themes that emerged from the discussion were as follows:

- Public humanities: many humanities scholars are increasingly interested in making their research "accessible and valuable" to the general public in nonacademic venues.
- Interdisciplinarity: the humanities are highly interdisciplinary, and scholars need training on methods and literature reviews of unfamiliar disciplines.

- Copyright: there is a lot of confusion around copyright issues, material reuse, and the open-access movement.
- Discovering and accessing special collections: this is key for humanities scholars, as these collections are the raw material for their research.[6]

Collections and Special Collections

Collections are important to scholars in the humanities and even beyond accessing library resources, these scholars often accumulate large amounts of materials in their private collections, which they often consult first when researching.[7] Engaging with your humanities departments requires a deep knowledge not only of your own library's collection and the research interests of the faculty in your departments, but also where those do not overlap. Is there a digitized collection of materials provided by a library vendor that can be purchased to assist your faculty? Universities often provide startup funds for their incoming science faculty to create the laboratory space they need for their research. Library collections are the humanities equivalent to that laboratory space, and it is exceedingly rare that humanities faculty startup funds include money to acquire them. As an engaged liaison in the humanities, you should be in conversation about humanities faculty's teaching and research needs with your collections department, or librarian, or whoever oversees the collections budget.

To experience how some liaisons have engaged with their humanities departments in the area of collections, see the stories by Alexis Pavenick, Kathia Salomé Ibacache Oliva, Greg Schmidt, and Joyce Martin. To learn how some liaisons have connected their collections to milestone dates and events to engage with faculty, see the stories by Patricia Brown, Jeanne Ewert, and Robert S. Means.

Individual Research

Be aware that your humanities faculty are most likely working on research individually. Coauthored or collaborative research is usually not prized when it comes to tenure and promotion. (An exception to this is in DH, which we will address a little later.) While they work individually, they do employ student research assistants, either at the graduate or undergraduate level, who will perform such tasks as "finding and retrieving secondary content provided by the scholar, conducting literature reviews, and transcribing oral history interviews."[8] Having a well-trained student assistant, then, is important. Ask the humanities faculty in your liaison department if they would like you to meet with their research assistants for this type of training. I (Ellen) once met with the graduate research assistant to a religious studies faculty member who wanted help with citation management for himself, but also so he could set up a good workflow for collecting secondary research materials for his faculty member and the other grad assistants in their research group.

Humanists and Information Professionals

The way that humanities research interact with information professionals is obviously of key interest. The Ithaka S+R report finds that researchers who engage with nondigitized primary source materials often have to go outside of their institutions to study them. They heavily rely on information professionals such as archivists and curators to help them access the materials needed for their research. Can you provide for your faculty a list of archives of literary or historical importance or provide introductions to other librarians, archivists, or curators? At their home institutions, humanists increasingly rely on librarians to partner with them in providing research assistance to graduates and undergraduates. However, it can be harder to scale this time of assistance, as each researcher may need individualized attention to find which archives or databases of primary sources will be applicable to their research. Therefore, setting aside time in your schedule to provide the necessary in-depth research assistance for these students is important.

To learn about how one liaison librarian in the humanities engages with faculty early in the process—while they are still on the job hunt—see the story by John Glover.

🌀 Digital Humanities

Another aspect of the MLA roundtable, which has also been reflected in other humanities professional associations (such as the American Historical Association and the American Academy of Religion) is the growing importance of DH. DH has been defined as:

> an area of scholarly activity at the intersection of computing or digital technologies and the disciplines of the humanities. It includes the systematic use of digital resources in the humanities, as well as the analysis of their application. DH can be defined as new ways of doing scholarship that involve collaborative, transdisciplinary, and computationally engaged research, teaching, and publishing. It brings digital tools and methods to the study of the humanities with the recognition that the printed word is no longer the main medium for knowledge production and distribution.[9]

While DH is a tremendous area of growth right now in humanities research, it can be intimidating for humanists to engage with the subdiscipline, not only because it requires new methodological lenses, but because they are then confronted with a dizzying array of technological tools that may be needed to do the research.

Over the last decade, academic libraries have increasingly been offering support for DH, as noted by Jaguszewski and Williams in their Association of Research Libraries report about changing roles for liaisons.[10] Many libraries have either retrained their humanities liaisons in support of the tools and methods of DH or hired additional DH "functional specialists" who have already had advanced training or experience. If your library does not have positions dedicated solely to digital scholarship, consider finding training opportunities to learn about DH methods and tools.

To understand how some liaisons have engaged with their faculty through DH, see the stories by Autumn Johnson and Caitlin Bagley.

CONTINUING EDUCATION AND TRAINING OPPORTUNITIES FOR THE DIGITAL HUMANITIES

- Digital Humanities Summer Institute (https://dhsi.org/)—intensive coursework during the summer, sponsored by the Electronic Textual Cultures Lab (https://etcl.uvic.ca/)
- Digital Humanities Research Institute (https://www.dhinstitutes.org/)—intensive summer coursework; network of local institutes across the United States.
- Digital Humanities Course Registry (https://dhcr.clarin-dariah.eu/courses)—an open online inventory of DH modules, courses, and programs in Europe and beyond that aims to help students, researchers, lecturers, and institutions to find, promote, and connect to teaching and training activities related to DH.

RELEVANT LIBRARY LISTSERVS IN THE HUMANITIES

- les-l@lists.ala.org (Literature in English Section Discussion List)
- acr-dgll@lists.ala.org (Association of College and Research Libraries [ACRL] Language and Linguistics Discussion Group)
- acr-historyig@lists.ala.org (ACRL History Librarians Interest Group)
- history-l@lists.ala.org (Reference and User Services Association History Section Discussion List)
- acr-historyig@lists.ala.org (ACRL History Librarians Interest Group)
- acr-dgprts@lists.ala.org (ACRL Philosophical, Religious, and Theological Studies Discussion Group)
- dss-dh_dg@lists.ala.org (ACRL Digital Scholarship Section Digital Humanities Discussion Group)
- anss-l@lists.ala.org (Anthropology and Sociology Section)

Stories can be read in the supplement at the publisher's website.
www.liaisonengagementsuccess.com

- Advocating for Books in Print—by Alexis Pavenick, California State University, Long Beach

    "In my experience as a liaison for the English Department, I find one key way to engage with faculty is to be an advocate for books in print. Perhaps, like my Collections Officer, some may wonder what it is about print books that keeps teachers of the humanities so enthralled. Why do they insist we buy print, in this day and age?"

- Latin American Indigenous Languages Collections—by Kathia Salomé Ibacache Oliva, University of Colorado Boulder

    "This story of engagement began when I was alerted to a collection gap concerning Latin American indigenous languages books. This sparked my interest, which led me to obtain a grant from the University of Colorado Boulder's Office of Diversity, Equity, and Community Engagement. The idea was to facilitate Latin American Indigenous Languages Literature through the creation of a collection and to advance scholarship and course curriculum."

- Special Collections Library Liaison Engagement: The Power of "Yes and"—by Greg Schmidt, Auburn University

    "The concept of 'yes and' comes from improvisational comedy in which participants are urged to accept what their partners have stated and expand on that line of thinking. Embracing the 'yes and' concept can lead participants in unexpected directions. For liaison engagement, 'yes and' can be a powerful concept, too. This is a story of how over the course of eight years of 'yes and' discussions two faculty transformed library instruction, received professional and materials funding, and expanded both teaching and special collections horizons."

- Fellowships for Special Collections Engagement—by Joyce Martin, Arizona State University

    "The goals of the fellowship program are significant: not only to promote the use of unique [Arizona State University] ASU Library collections, but also to provide a positive contribution to the issues of racism, oppression, and violence in the West. Each fellowship provides $2,500 to support a short-term research visit for an established scholar, a PhD candidate, or postdoctoral student to use vital ASU Library primary and rare secondary sources to aid in the applicant's research."

- Connecting Special Collections to the Digital Humanities—by Autumn Johnson, Georgia Southern University

    "Special Collections instruction requests often include requests to incorporate the library's rarest materials into sessions. This includes our modest collection of early printed books and a single fifteenth-century handwritten manuscript. Recently, liaison faculty in Digital Humanities expressed renewed interest in these materials, hoping to connect the history of the printed book and their disciplinary field in a more meaningful way."

- Hand on the Net: Helping Land Job Candidates for Liaison Departments—by John Glover, Virginia Commonwealth University

"Meeting with liaison department job candidates, whatever the encounter's format, provides multiple points of engagement with liaison departments."
- Classical Virtual Reality—by Caitlin Bagley, Gonzaga University

  "Ultimately, this project involved working with all departments of the library, bringing students in for research help, and created lasting contacts that paid off in future semesters through students returning to the library for projects unrelated to the first."
- A Practical Story about Public Poetry—by Patricia Brown, Northwestern State University

  "How do we as liaison librarians reach through overfilled workdays to engage the larger university? Although the subtle method of liaison described herein does not make a big splash in quantitative assessment metrics, it does show how shared academic or artistic activity might encourage department faculty and students to see their mutual interests as a bridge between their work and the library."
- Milestone Anniversaries Celebrating Authors—by Jeanne Ewert, University of Florida

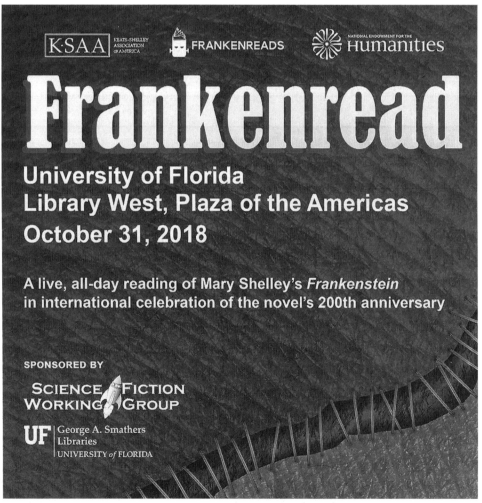

Figure 5.1. Frankenread promotional graphic from the George A. Smathers Libraries, University of Florida. *Photo credit: Stephanie Birch*

"As the English and American Literature librarian at the University of Florida, an engaging and rewarding form of outreach for me has been public celebrations of significant anniversaries of authors' lives and work."

- World War I Events and Exhibits—by Robert S. Means, Brigham Young University

    "Not all years will provide such centennials just waiting to be observed, but I've learned to keep a folder that looks ahead at upcoming 'anniversaries' of events, authors' birth and death dates, [and] book publication dates, so that I'll be prepared with enough time to get in the queue for an exhibit, to propose a class, or just to get on the busy schedule of the teaching faculty who might want to collaborate on 'something.'"

Key Points

- The humanist's laboratories are library collections, which makes them key partners with librarians.
- The MLA has determined that the top issues for humanities research are (1) public humanities, (2) interdisciplinarity, (3) copyright, (4) discovering and accessing special collections and archives, and (5) the burgeoning field of DH.
- DH is blossoming, but many humanists still aren't trained on its methods and tools.
- Liaisons to the humanities should work closely with their digital scholarship colleagues, or retrain to help support DH initiatives.

Notes

1. Rachel Ivy Clarke and Young-In Kim, "The More Things Change, the More They Stay the Same: Educational and Disciplinary Backgrounds of American Librarians, 1950–2015," *Journal of Education for Library and Information Science* 59, no. 4 (October 2018): 179–205, https://doi.org/10.3138/jelis.59.4.2018-0001.

2. Rens Bod, *A New History of the Humanities: The Search for Principles and Patterns from Antiquity to the Present* (Oxford University Press, 2013), 1, https://www.oxfordscholarship.com/view/10.1093/acprof:oso/9780199665211.001.0001/acprof-9780199665211.

3. "Humanities," *Wikipedia*, February 5, 2020, https://en.wikipedia.org/w/index.php?title=Humanities&oldid=939203973.

4. Danielle Cooper and Roger Schonfeld, "Rethinking Liaison Programs for the Humanities" (Ithaka S+R, July 26, 2017), 6–8, https://doi.org/10.18665/sr.304124.

5. Mary Onorato et al., "What Is Humanities Research Now?" (2020 MLA Annual Convention, MLA, 2020), https://mla.confex.com/mla/2020/meetingapp.cgi/Session/6465.

6. Onorato et al., "What Is Humanities Research Now?"

7. Stephen K Stoan, "Research and Information Retrieval among Academic Researchers: Implications for Library Instruction," *Library Trends* 39, no. 3 (1991): 238–57.

8. Cooper and Schonfeld, "Rethinking Liaison Programs for the Humanities," 7.

9. "Digital Humanities," *Wikipedia*, February 13, 2020, https://en.wikipedia.org/w/index.php?title=Digital_humanities&oldid=940570346.

10. Janice Jaguszewski and Karen Williams, "New Roles for New Times: Transforming Liaison Roles in Research Libraries" (Association of Research Libraries, 2013), http://conservancy.umn.edu/handle/11299/169867.

CHAPTER 6

Engagement with the Social Sciences

IN THIS CHAPTER

▷ What are the social sciences?

▷ How do social scientists research?

○ Information-seeking process
○ Using data in research

▷ Stories of engagement in the social sciences

THE SOCIAL SCIENCES ARE THE HOME of the academic disciplines of library and information science (LIS) (even though LIS is also a profession; see chapter 9), so many librarians may feel a natural affinity as a liaison to disciplines in this area. However, education in social science research methods is not standard among LIS master's programs: some programs do not require a research methods class; the content of the classes that exist can vary considerably; and many practitioner librarians either do not have the time, the support, or the desire to pursue research as a part of their jobs, even if they were required to complete a course.[1] In addition, many research methods courses in LIS programs focus on the needs of LIS doctoral students, which is not necessarily focused on the practitioner research many librarians undertake.[2] Nevertheless, librarians usually have had at least some exposure to discussing qualitative and quantitative methods, survey design, and basic statistical analysis, and these are the hallmarks of social science research. Therefore, in being a liaison to a social science discipline there may be a common ground of understanding.

What Are the Social Sciences?

The Columbia Encyclopedia defines the *social sciences* as "any or all branches of study that deal with humans in their social relations."[3] The social science disciplines gain knowledge through empirical or scientific methods, the major methods being observation, interviews, surveys, and case studies. Data collected can be both quantitative and qualitative. Social science research can often be directly practical to the real world, and researchers are often called on to advise educational institutions, government, and industry with their planning and development.

TRADITIONAL SOCIAL SCIENCE DISCIPLINES[4]

- Anthropology (can also be considered a part of the humanities)
- Business (can also be considered a professional discipline)
- Communication studies
- Economics
- Education (can also be considered a professional discipline)
- Geography
- History (can also be considered a part of the humanities)
- Law (can also be considered a part of the humanities or a professional discipline)
- Linguistics
- Political science
- Psychology (can also be considered a science)
- Sociology

ADDITIONAL SOCIAL SCIENCE DISCIPLINES (NOT COMPREHENSIVE):

- Archaeology
- Area studies
- Criminal justice
- Environmental studies
- Ethnic studies
- Information science
- International studies
- Library science
- Public policy
- Women's and gender studies

To read about how some liaison librarians have engaged with students and faculty in their areas by connecting social science research to the community, the country, and the world, see the stories by Kian Flynn, Chelsea Nesvig, and Abby Moore.

ⓖ How Do Social Scientists Research?

Social scientists' information-seeking and research behaviors have been well-documented in the literature.[5] In the 1970s, information scientists published a landmark study on social scientists' use of and need for information. This study discovered that social scientists:

- Found it important to trace information through citations.
- Found information formally through journals.
- Found information informally through their network of colleagues and experts.
- Did not use the services of librarians or library resources often to find information.[6]

While social scientists consider library journal purchasing to be essential to their research, they have not always seen librarian expertise as needed because their own disciplinary networks were sufficient. A 1989 study of social scientists' information use behaviors documented similar findings, with the caveat that pre–preliminary exam graduate students in the social sciences relied on librarians for literature searching, perhaps because they did not yet have the networks of colleagues through which more experienced social scientists found such information.[7] A 2018 Ithaka S+R faculty survey found that social scientists were the most likely to start their literature searching not using library resources but instead using Google Scholar or a general-purpose search engine.[8]

To learn how a liaison librarian embedded himself into the world of social science research through a degree program, see the story by Amit Doshi.

Information-seeking Process

Social scientists participate in several types of activities when they are looking for information. These activities, identified by Meho and Tibbo,[9] are listed here:

1. Starting—at the beginning of a research project, they search the literature for an overview of or background information about the topic. They read journal articles, newspaper articles, and interview colleagues. While they sometimes search library databases, as documented in previous studies, many social scientists start a literature search with their own collection of articles or journals. Some social scientists have indicated that they contact librarians for help during this stage.
2. Chaining—this activity refers to following references that they glean from reading articles. For librarians, who are familiar with citation indexes or the "cited by" feature of Google Scholar, finding other references for researchers can be a great way to assist them during this type of information seeking.
3. Browsing—this activity is similar to chaining, in that it is still seeking out more information on the original topic, but it comes through browsing through tables of contents of journals or books, or through online catalogs and databases.

4. Monitoring—this activity keeps up the social scientist's awareness of a topic, by reading listservs and journals, attending conferences, and talking with their network of colleagues.

5. Accessing—this activity, which is a lynchpin in the information seeking process, means actually acquiring the texts of the materials needed. When this breaks down, further activities are harder to accomplish. Librarians who implement link resolvers and support robust interlibrary loan programs can definitely be of service in this area.

6. Differentiating—this activity should seem familiar to any librarian who teaches information literacy, as it involves evaluating resources for credibility, bias, and relevance.

7. Extracting—this activity involves searching through resources to find specific information or data.

8. Verifying—this is another evaluative activity, specifically checking for accuracy.

9. Networking—this activity involves communicating with others, not just for information gathering, but also for information dissemination. Librarians can and should be a part of a researcher's network to give the best information about this task.

10. Information managing—this activity includes archiving and organizing the information they have found. This is, again, another area where librarian assistance is key, whether they assist with citation management software or data management planning. Managing information is what librarians have trained to do.

Hopefully, through describing the types of information seeking activities that social scientists take part in, librarians who are liaisons to social science departments can see where promoting their services, expertise, and resources can intervene in ways to help these researchers. With recent trends in social science research, researchers may be in need of more support than ever.

Using Data in Research

Social scientists have always collected and analyzed data, both quantitative and qualitative, and in this era of "big data," when data on people's activity is produced with such volume, the need for social scientists to access and analyze this data has become paramount.[10] Libraries that provide digital scholarship services and can train researchers on data access, data management, digital methodologies, and data visualization can support groundbreaking social science research.

As the liaison to a department of journalism, I (Ellen) have seen how my faculty use both traditional and social media data in their research. As I work in partnership with our digital scholarship librarian (who is helpfully situated organizationally in our library's department that includes the liaison program) I have learned, for example, what the archive limitations for harvesting Twitter data are and so have trained the faculty who publish on social media topics to collect Twitter posts in the early process of formulating a research idea. This can sometimes seem a little backward to researchers, who are used to formulating a research question before deciding on a methodology and plan for collecting data. But methodological considerations become limited if you are unable to collect data at all, so it is important to understanding the scope of how, or even *if*, the data that you need can be collected.

Knowing how to help your researchers formulate data management plans can be useful for social science liaisons as well because the National Science Foundation (NSF) and the National Institutes of Health (NIH), the largest of the funders that require data management plans, also award grants in the social sciences. Mandates for data sharing have spurred important discussions around how data is archived and reused, particularly when it involves data from human subjects.[11] Libraries, which have answered the need for data services in the university over the last decade, specifically for data management planning and data archiving,[12] should be proactive in engaging with their faculty researchers over this issue, which puts the liaison front and center in this work. There is more discussion on the liaison's role in research data management in the chapter on engagement with the STEM fields (Chapter 7), but it is important to note here that this work is also important for social science liaisons.

To consider how some liaison librarians have engaged their faculty with data and data visualization, see the stories by Jesse Klein, Susan E. Montgomery, and Laura Wimberley.

RELEVANT LIBRARY LISTSERVS IN THE SOCIAL SCIENCES:

- anss-l@lists.ala.org (Anthropology and Sociology Section of the Association of College and Research Libraries [ACRL])
- wgss-l@lists.ala.org (Women and Gender Studies Section of ACRL)
- ebss-l@lists.ala.org (Education and Behavioral Sciences Section of ACRL)
- comlib-l@lists.illinois.edu (Communications Librarians Discussion List)
- listserv@listserv.kent.edu (Politics, Policy, and International Relations)
- ifla-soc-lib@iflalists.org (Forum of the International Federation of Library Associations and Institutions Social Science Libraries section)

Stories of Engagement in the Social Sciences

Stories can be read in the supplement at the publisher's website.
www.liaisonengagementsuccess.com

- Health Data Stories Using Infographics—by Jesse Klein, Florida State University
    "Both as a data librarian and a sociologist, I really enjoy making data discovery, storytelling, and visualization more accessible to students. Infographics provide a medium through which to engage students in data, statistical, and visual literacy and make them more informed consumers of information. This liaison and embedded instruction experience has been incredibly rewarding and I'm excited to continue working with students in future semesters to bring these health policy narratives to life."

- Developing Data Skills in Political Science Using ArcGIS—by Susan E. Montgomery, Rollins College

   "As information expands, librarians learn new content and skills. This learning helps us better serve users. As the library liaison to the Political Science department at our college, I have been able to share my knowledge and interest in data visualization with my colleagues as well as support them in their endeavors to incorporate new content and skills into their courses."

- "What Motivates You?" Liaison Work with Human Rights Seminar Students in Washington, DC—by Chelsea Nesvig, University of Washington Bothell

   "Liaison librarians are resources: eager, helpful, and creative. We work hard to ensure that the research and information needs of students and faculty are being met while they are on campus or in the library. Yet when student work is being done off-campus, that relationship shifts, and librarians can have the opportunity to consider how best to meet students' research needs outside of the library."

Figure 6.1. Liaison Librarian Chelsea Nesvig in Washington, DC, with students. *Photo credit: Chelsea Nesvig*

- Global Engagement: Liaison Librarianship on Campus and Beyond—by Abby Moore, University of North Carolina at Charlotte

  "Building relationships is a vital part of a liaison librarian's job and can lead to meaningful opportunities that may not be included in our job descriptions. Answering that first email from the Honors College was the first step in establishing a relationship that has changed my job in fantastic and unforeseen ways."

- Connecting Research to the Community—by Kian Flynn, University of Washington

  "Though I work as a librarian for a public university and frequently answer reference questions from members of the public, planning for this exhibit was one of the first times in my three years in my current role when I felt like I engaged in substantive collaboration with an organization outside of the university. It was a welcomed and meaningful change."

- Transcending "Us" and "Them"—by Ameet Doshi, Georgia Institute of Technology

  "I submit that obtaining a doctorate within the discipline I serve is a very intense path to gain insight into the inner workings of students and faculty. After all, I could have just deployed a survey or convened focus groups to get a sense of what 'they' want. But I would never trade the knowledge gained within the classroom, as well as through interactions with students and faculty, for a more passive path to user-centered insight."

- Outreach Events as Liaison Work—by Laura Wimberley, California State University Northridge

  "These events will ultimately help your professional development: you will know the faculty better as people and learn more facets of the field and its cutting-edge research. And as a bonus, you can even enjoy yourself at a fun event."

⊚ Key Points

- Social scientists use the scientific method to study social or human phenomena, and often connect their work to solving human problems.
- Social scientists depend on scholarly journals for their research, but often don't use librarians as resources in favor of their professional network.
- There are places in the social science information-seeking process where the assistance of a liaison librarian would be helpful.
- Data is an area where social scientists may need librarian expertise. Librarians can help them with data finding, accessing, managing, archiving, and visualizing.

⊚ Notes

1. Lili Luo, "Fusing Research into Practice: The Role of Research Methods Education," *Library and Information Science Research* 33, no. 3 (July 1, 2011): 191–201, https://doi.org/10.1016/j.lisr.2010.12.001.

2. Marie Kennedy and Kristine Brancolini, "Academic Librarian Research: A Survey of Attitudes, Involvement, and Perceived Capabilities," *College and Research Libraries* 73, no. 5 (2012): 431–48.

3. Paul Lagasse, "Social Science," *The Columbia Encyclopedia* (New York: Columbia University Press, August 1, 2018), http://search.credoreference.com/content/entry/columency/social _science/0.

4. "Social Science," *Wikipedia*, February 24, 2020, https://en.wikipedia.org/w/index.php ?title=Social_science&oldid=942401311.

5. David Ellis, "A Behavioural Approach to Information Retrieval System Design," *Journal of Documentation*, 1989; Lokman I. Meho and Helen R. Tibbo, "Modeling the Information-Seeking Behavior of Social Scientists: Ellis's Study Revisited," *Journal of the American Society for Information Science and Technology* 54, no. 6 (2003): 570–87, https://doi.org/10.1002/asi.10244; Mary B. Folster, "Information Seeking Patterns: Social Sciences," *The Reference Librarian* 23, no. 49–50 (1995): 83–93.

6. Maurice B. Line, "The Information Uses and Needs of Social Scientists: An Overview of INFROSS," *ASLIB Proceedings; London* 23, no. 8 (August 1, 1971): 412.

7. Mary B. Folster, "A Study of the Use of Information by Social Science Researchers," *Journal of Academic Librarianship* 15, no. 1 (March 1989): 7.

8. Melissa Blankstein and Christine Wolff-Eisenberg, "Ithaka S+R US Faculty Survey 2018" (Ithaka S+R, April 12, 2019), https://doi.org/10.18665/sr.311199.

9. Meho and Tibbo, "Modeling the Information-Seeking Behavior of Social Scientists."

10. Marta Stelmaszak and Philipp Hukal, "When Data Science Meets Social Sciences: The Benefits of the Data Revolution Are Clear but Careful Reflection Is Needed," *Impact of Social Sciences* (blog), March 1, 2017, https://blogs.lse.ac.uk/impactofsocialsciences/2017/03/01/when -data-science-meets-social-sciences-the-benefits-of-the-data-revolution-are-clear-but-careful -reflection-is-needed/.

11. Louise Corti, "Re-Using Archived Qualitative Data—Where, How, Why?" *Archival Science* 7, no. 1 (March 1, 2007): 37–54, https://doi.org/10.1007/s10502-006-9038-y; Renata Curty et al., "Untangling Data Sharing and Reuse in Social Sciences," *Proceedings of the Association for Information Science and Technology* 53, no. 1 (2016): 1–5, https://doi.org/10.1002/pra2.2016.14505301025.

12. Sheila Corrall, "Roles and Responsibilities: Libraries, Librarians and Data," in *Managing Research Data*, ed. Graham Pryor (Facet London, 2012), 105–133; David Fearon Jr. et al., "Research Data Management Services," SPEC Kit (Association of Research Libraries, August 1, 2013), https://publications.arl.org/Research-Data-Management-Services-SPEC-Kit-334/.

Engagement with the STEM Fields

LIBRARIANS HAVE A STEREOTYPE ABOUT SCIENTISTS that they are usually secluded in their actual laboratories and hardly ever enter the physical library. While many librarians know exceptions to this stereotype, it is still important to acknowledge that the internet fundamentally changed the way that scientists interact with the library. As articles and conference proceedings have increasingly been published online, the need to access physical materials from the library space has decreased. Providing seamless access to these materials will always be a needed library service, and perhaps one that needs better PR, but in recent years, libraries have been innovating to find new ways of providing research support services to science researchers.

To find out how some liaison librarians are engaging their faculty and staff with outreach events, see the stories by Stephanie Pierce and Aida Almanza.

⊙ What Are the Sciences?

The *Columbia Encyclopedia* defines *science* as "the organized body of knowledge concerning the physical world, both animate and inanimate" but it is important to note that a more specific definition would need to include the methods by which scientific knowledge is acquired. The scientific method is a set of steps that includes (1) gathering information or data by observation, (2) forming a hypothesis based on that information, (3) testing that hypothesis through further information and experimentation, and (4) drawing conclusions based on the results of the experimentation.[1] Different disciplines or subdisciplines of science may have different ways of carrying out their experimentation, but the overarching characteristic of scientists is the fundamental adherence to the scientific method.

⊙ What Is STEM?

STEM is an acronym that stands for *science, technology, engineering, and math*, and is a term that groups together those academic disciplines. This term has been used since the early 2000s, and was popularized by the National Science Foundation (NSF), which used the acronym to discuss education policy and curriculum for those disciplines collectively.[2] While the engineering and technology fields owe a lot to science and the scientific method, practitioners and researchers in those fields tend to use the engineering design process, which moves through an iterative process wherein they "ask questions, imagine solutions, plan designs, create and test models, and then make improvements."[3] Engineers ask the questions, "How do I solve this problem?" and "How can I make it better?"

To learn about how some liaison librarians are engaging their campus with an engineering staple—the makerspace—see the story by Zachary W. Painter, Joseph Makokha, and Michael Nack.

TRADITIONAL STEM DISCIPLINES[4]

- Mathematics
- Statistics
- Physical sciences
  - Physics
  - Chemistry
  - Astronomy
- Earth sciences
  - Geology
  - Paleontology

- ○ Oceanography
- ○ Meteorology
- • Life sciences
  - ○ Biology
  - ○ Botany
  - ○ Zoology
  - ○ Genetics
  - ○ Medicine
- • Applied sciences
  - ○ Engineering
    - ▪ Mechanical
    - ▪ Civil
    - ▪ Aeronautical
    - ▪ Electrical
    - ▪ Chemical
  - ○ Agronomy
  - ○ Horticulture
  - ○ Medicine (Allied health disciplines can also be considered a profession)
- • Psychology (can also be considered a social science)

How Do Scientists Research?

Scientists define *research* as the systematic investigation of theories and hypotheses tested through experiments in which data is collected and analyzed. Scientific research happens mainly in a laboratory or while doing fieldwork. This can sometimes be at odds with how many librarians use the word *research*, which often has a bent toward the humanist or social science way of thinking. Research to a scientist is clearly not just reading books in a library or searching through the journal databases; however, this does not mean that scientists do not need the library for their research. Scholarly research in the sciences builds on previous knowledge, and being able to search and retrieve the literature where that knowledge is found is an important step in scientific research. It is in this area that scientists interact with traditional library services.

Information Seeking and the Internet

A 2007 study of scientists' information-seeking behavior found that they first prefer to search specific disciplinary scholarly databases, followed by the use of Google Scholar, which tends to produce the type of information they are looking for, mainly scholarly journals.[5] A more recent study has found, however, that early career scientific researchers tend to use Google Scholar before any other platform for searching, although they often need to use library resources for accessing the full-text documents.[6] According to that same study, despite Google Scholar's dominance, Web of Science and Scopus continue to be popular when searching for information, but also for determining journal impact factors.[7]

As stated previously, scientists in academia adopted internet technology early for many reasons, but the need to access and communicate scientific information was a primary driver.[8] The need for quick and easy ways of accessing and disseminating scientific information has meant that scientists have always been innovators when it comes to new scholarly communication initiatives. They paved the way for the modern open-access movement by founding some of the first freely available journals and books published on the internet. The physics online repository arXiv.org was an early pioneer in archiving freely available preprints of scholarly journal articles. Having preprints freely available before publication means that other scientists can access your research without the delay of the peer-review and publication process and can allow peer feedback right away.

To discover how a liaison librarian engaged with her faculty by partnering with database vendors, see the story by Kimberly Reycraft.

PREPRINT REPOSITORIES IN THE SCIENCES

- arXiv.org (physics, mathematics, computer science, quantitative biology, quantitative finance, statistics, electrical engineering and systems science, economics)
- bioRxiv.org (biological and life sciences)
- medRxiv.org (health sciences, dentistry, nursing, pharmacology, physical therapy)
- engrXiv.org (engineering, computer science)
- TechRxiv.org (technical research in electrical engineering, computer science, and related areas)
- OSF Preprints (multiple scientific disciplines, also includes social science and humanities)
- Preprints.org (multiple scientific disciplines, also includes social science and humanities)

Data and Data Management

In the past decade, as academic libraries have started to redefine services to support researcher needs, one issue that has come to the forefront is the need for research data management. Academic libraries providing data management services came about around the time that research funders, such as the NSF and the National Institutes of Medicine, started requiring data management plans (DMP) as a part of the proposal submission process. These DMPs include information about how the researchers will manage and disseminate the physical and digital data generated by their research. What type of data will be generated, and in what format will it be stored? Is that format accessible and, if not, are there ways to make it accessible? How will the data be disseminated? Where will it be disseminated from and what metadata or code needs to be available to guide others in accessing it? How can the data be reused or reproduced? And finally, how will the data be archived and preserved for the future? These questions connect in so many ways to the work that libraries do with all types of information: collecting, storing, managing, describing, allowing access to, and disseminating. That is why libraries have embraced research data management services and many science liaisons have partnered with this effort.

Life Cycle of Research

Many libraries have begun to realize that the need for services from the library extend across the full life cycle of research, and this has put a bright spotlight on STEM research specifically. While data services may be one conspicuous point of need, there are other points on the cycle as well: early ones, like the grant planning and development process, and later ones, like research preservation and dissemination.

At North Carolina State University, STEM librarians developed a program of embedding into the weekly lab meetings of research groups. This way they were able to offer library and data services at the point of need, and much earlier in the life cycle of STEM research. They discovered that in almost 60 percent of the meetings they attended, the librarians were able to provide point-of-need expertise on everything from guidance designing a literature search, data management assistance, to knowledge about publishing and research impact. Because of this program, they learned that "offering librarian expertise and a library's services within researchers' authentic workflows transforms research support services from just-in-case, contextless, library-centered services into point-of-need, authentic, contextualized, user-centered services."[9]

To appreciate how some liaisons have partnered with their institution's research enterprise unit to support researchers along the full life cycle of their research, see the story by Rachel Martinez and Matthew Harp.

Scholarly Metrics

Science liaison librarians should be aware of the needs of the science researchers in their departments, not just for data management services, but also for assistance in the area of scholarly metrics, such as H-index, journal impact factor, acceptance rates, and number of citations, among others. While scholarly metrics are sometimes used in hiring decisions or in deciding where to allocate resources,[10] the science disciplines more often than not encourage or require their use in the process of tenure and promotion, and many researchers turn to their liaison for assistance in producing these metrics.[11] The level of support you bring to providing scholarly metrics for your faculty or departments (point-of-need assistance, education, or dedicated staff) may depend on the size of the library or administrative mandates, but it is imperative for STEM liaisons to have a proficient level of knowledge in this area.

Functional Specialists

Liaison librarianship has begun moving toward functional or hybrid liaison models, for which services such as scholarly communication, data management, copyright, scholarly metrics, data visualization, or geographic information systems become the individualized function of specialist liaisons. This has put a spotlight on science liaisons, specifically whether or not there will be a need for subject specialization in science liaison work. In a recent survey of science liaisons, researchers found that:

> science librarians generally perceive that the liaison relationship with departments is a valuable and necessary component of academic science librarianship, and that subject specialization benefits this relationship. Many respondents believe that newer functional roles, such as scholarly communication and research data management, will continue to grow and will become more important in the future, but that liaison relationships will remain necessary for these services to succeed. [Their] results suggest, albeit inconclusively, that there may be a trend toward a more generalist approach to liaison librarianship, with science librarians acting as liaisons to multiple departments and subject areas.[12]

This research found that science liaisons believe that functional roles can only be built on the relationships and departmental connections that exist through subject liaison work.

To read a story of a well-rounded approach to STEM liaison librarianship, see the story by Innocent Awasom.

RELEVANT LIBRARY LISTSERVS IN STEM

- sts-l@lists.ala.org (Association of College and Research Libraries [ACRL] Science and Technology Section Discussion List)
- eldnet-l@u.washington.edu (Engineering Libraries Division of American Society for Engineering Education)
- medref@lists.ala.org (Reference Services Section Health and Medical Reference)
- acrl-hsig@lists.purdue.edu (Health Sciences Interest Group of ACRL)

Stories can be read in the supplement at the publisher's website.
www.liaisonengagementsuccess.com

- Gathering around the Table: Promoting community and relationship building in STEM Disciplines—by Stephanie Pierce, University of Arkansas

  "I view the 'Breakfast with Your Library' events as a way to show my liaison departments that the University of Arkansas Libraries and I view them as multidimensional people whom we are here to support both academically and personally through inviting spaces, encouraging community building across departments and campus, and establishing the library as an integral support structure socially and academically while they are part of our campus community."

- Chemistry Lotería—by Aida Almanza, Texas A&M University San Antonio

  "I think this nontraditional form of outreach increased my connection to the department because now faculty feel more comfortable reaching out to me with questions or book requests. It also set the stage for future partnerships and inspired the other liaisons to reach out to student clubs and organizations. For students, events like this make them realize the library can be a fun place too."

Figure 7.1. Jaguar Isotopes Chemistry Club, attendees, and Aida Almanza, the Arts and Sciences Librarian, posing at the end of the event. *Photo credit: Aida Almanza*

Figure 7.2. Chemistry Lotería table. *Photo credit: Aida Almanza*

- Partnering with Publishers for STEM Database Awareness—by Kimberly Reycraft, Florida Gulf Coast University

  "Many publishers and vendors have client services managers or similar employees on staff who are happy to partner with librarians to provide these types of events. Once the logistics are set up, simply put on your name tag, smile, and enjoy engaging with the students and faculty you serve!"

- The Mobile Maker Cart: A Rolling Makerspace Concept—by Zachary W. Painter, Joseph Makokha, and Michael Nack, Stanford University

  "We initially targeted people who either had no experience with using makerspace items, or who wanted to take items into an alternate space to practice rapid prototyping. If they needed more sophisticated equipment, they could then more confidently go to a full-featured makerspace after using our Mobile Maker Cart (MMC)."

- Partnering with Knowledge Enterprise Research Support Staff—by Rachel Martinez and Matthew Harp, Arizona State University

  "Our reason for partnering with [Knowledge Enterprise's] RAs was to promote our skills and services to researchers who were looking to secure funding and ultimately gain more visibility in the sphere of research at [Arizona State University]."

- STEM Librarians in the Triple Helix Mix—by Innocent Awasom, Texas Tech University

  "Library liaisons provide support or subject matter expertise and play a critical role in linking faculty, staff, students and community users to scholarly resources for research, instruction, outreach, knowledge use/creation and dissemination purposes. We build and maintain mutually beneficial scholarly relationships, thus fulfilling the triple helix of Research, Instruction, and Outreach/Engagement."

⊚ Key Points

- Scientists perform lab and field research and use the library for literature searching.
- Scientists have pioneered technology-driven innovation in scholarly communication, and often deposit their open-access publications in preprint archives and repositories.
- Data research services have become an important aspect of science liaison work.
- STEM liaisons should have a proficient knowledge of how scholarly metrics work.
- STEM liaisons need to look at the full life cycle of the research process to see where researcher needs exist.

⊚ Notes

1. Paul Lagasse, "Science," *The Columbia Encyclopedia* (New York: Columbia University Press, August 1, 2018), http://search.credoreference.com/content/entry/columency/social_science/0; "Scientific Method," *Wikipedia*, April 28, 2020, https://en.wikipedia.org/w/index.php?title=Scientific_method&oldid=953701752.

2. "Science, Technology, Engineering, and Mathematics," *Wikipedia*, April 26, 2020, https://en.wikipedia.org/w/index.php?title=Science,_technology,_engineering,_and_mathematics&oldid=953201346.

3. Sandra May, "Engineering Design Process," NASA, July 17, 2017, http://www.nasa.gov/audience/foreducators/best/edp.html.

4. Lagasse, "Science."

5. Christine Wolff, Alisa B. Rod, and Roger C Schonfeld, "Ithaka S+R US Faculty Survey 2015," 2015, 83.

6. David Nicholas et al., "Where and How Early Career Researchers Find Scholarly Information," *Learned Publishing* 30, no. 1 (2017): 19–29, https://doi.org/10.1002/leap.1087.

7. Nicholas et al., "Where and How."

8. Bradley M. Hemminger et al., "Information Seeking Behavior of Academic Scientists," *Journal of the American Society for Information Science and Technology* 58, no. 14 (2007): 2205–25, https://doi.org/10.1002/asi.20686.

9. Alexander J. Carroll, Honora N. Eskridge, and Bertha P. Chang, "Lab-Integrated Librarians: A Model for Research Engagement," *College and Research Libraries* 81, no. 1 (2020), https://doi.org/10.5860/crl.81.1.8.

10. Alison Abbott et al., "Do Metrics Matter?" *Nature* 465, no. 7300 (June 17, 2010): 860–63.

11. Dan DeSanto and Aaron Nichols, "Scholarly Metrics Baseline: A Survey of Faculty Knowledge, Use, and Opinion about Scholarly Metrics," *College and Research Libraries* 78, no. 2 (2017), https://doi.org/10.5860/crl.78.2.150.

12. Laura Bolton Palumbo, Jeffra D. Bussmann, and Barbara Kern, "The Value of Subject Specialization and the Future of Science Liaison Librarianship," *College and Research Libraries*, 2021, 21, https://doi.org/10.7282/T3-6B34-DK85.

Engagement in the Arts

WHILE FORMAL EDUCATION IN THE ARTS would likely benefit someone with arts-specific liaison assignments, it is certainly not required. For liaisons serving a variety of disciplines within the arts, the prospect of having formal education in such a wide scope of diverse domains is unlikely. As noted elsewhere in the book, having a discipline-related degree does not guarantee that a liaison will have complete understanding of the research needs in that field. As an example, a liaison with an undergraduate degree in theatre performance would not automatically be fully equipped to understand the needs of theatre history faculty members and how best to support them. This does not diminish the value of discipline-specific experience or education for the liaison, and it is quite possible to be a successful liaison to an area for which you have no formal training. As with other disciplinary assignments, liaisons should explore relevant professional associations and email lists or listservs, whether focused on the particular arts areas or specific to librarianship in those arts disciplines.

For a new liaison to the arts or a veteran liaison with new assignments, it's helpful to explore the discipline. The arts include a broad range of creative domains that are often subdivided in a variety of ways, with fluid or overlapping boundaries. Historically, the term *fine arts* referred to art forms created with the express purpose of exploring aesthetics, in contrast with decorative (or applied) arts created for utilitarian function, such as pottery or furniture.[1] Traditionally, fine arts include painting, sculpture, and architecture (despite its role as a functional art) as well as music and poetry. Often you will see terminology that groups related arts forms such as the performing arts (theatre, opera, or dance) or visual arts (painting, sculpture, printmaking, or photography) with distinction between those arts that are focused on performance as the art form versus those focused on the creation of artifact. This does, however, get messy. Film is a good example of this. Even though acting and performative work is taking place, the goal of film is to create an artifact, the film, and in this way, the film object is more similar to a painting or a sculpture. While film shares techniques and objects with other disciplines like journalism, such as documentary films, film fits among the other art forms when considering the earlier definition of *art* as that which is created for the express purpose of exploring aesthetics. Other groups might, on one level, appear to help clarify, but can just as often muddy the waters. Decorative arts include furniture that has the functional role of providing a place to sit or a table on which to eat or work, but artists have often stretched beyond the confines of the practical to explore aesthetics of design. Folk art and fine art each have their own distinctions, but also have commonalities in their tools, materials, or mediums. It is worth noting that some of the distinctions made among art forms are the product of the culture in which the art was created or the result of culturally established norms or perspectives. For example, western European arts traditions make the distinction between fine and decorative arts, but this is often less apparent or relevant in other cultures. The point is that it's important to discern the local meaning of the language you encounter, not only in the larger culture, but then also in the more specific culture of the institution in which you work. Be careful not to make assumptions or have preconceived notions about how a departmental culture views and defines their domain.

STUDIO AND CREATIVE ARTS DISCIPLINES

This is by no means exhaustive, but rather representational of the types of arts and terminology you may encounter:

- Visual arts—including two dimensional (painting, printmaking, photography) and three dimensional (sculpture, ceramics and pottery, fiber arts, architecture)
- Performing arts (music, dance, music, musical theatre, opera)
- Performance art (sometimes contrasted with traditional performing arts and growing out of visual arts, often including mixed media or interactive two-dimensional and three-dimensional art forms)
- Electronic media (film, animation, digital, computer art, design)

What Does Arts Research Look Like?

As you might expect, research in the arts can and does include traditional types of scholarship found in other disciplines and results in traditional research products like books and articles; for example, think of the scholarship related to the theory and history of any of the arts. Because this type of research is more generally represented in other disciplines, we will not expound on it here, but instead address other modalities of scholarship present in, but not exclusive to, the arts.

Types of Research Unique to the Arts

Practice-based and practice-led research is particularly prevalent in the creative arts and places primary importance on the practice of the art form. The byproducts of this kind of research are often musical compositions, performances, and visual artwork, among others, but equally important is the creative process from which these works are born.[2] Artistic inquiry as part of the research process has been documented in the literature early in the twentieth century.[3] Authors Barone and Eisner have contributed a most helpful resource for understanding what is and what isn't arts-based research in their book *Arts Based Research*, in which they contextualize this type of scholarship with a number of illuminating examples. About this kind of research, they note, "It is not simply a quantitative disclosure of an array of variables. It is the conscious pursuit of expressive form in the service of understanding."[4] It's worth noting here the distinction between arts-based research and research-based art: "Arts-based research uses the arts as a foundation for creating expressive forms that enlighten. Research-based art is the use of research in any modality that will serve as a basis for creating a work of art."[5]

For examples of how arts liaison librarians are embracing the connection between research and creativity, see stories by Bria Sinnott, Nimisha Bhat, and Andi Back.

So what does this mean for a liaison supporting arts faculty and programs? It means you will need to think creatively about how you can support other types of research modalities. It may involve some experimenting and openness to things that don't seem to fit nicely in predefined, traditional categories of research. It may raise challenges related to how you and the research community view the products of scholarship. Many institutions are wrestling with the uncertainty about how to "count" creative arts–based research and this has been the subject of a recent grant and study by a team of Baylor University librarians investigating alternative metrics for this kind of research among faculty members and their institutions.[6]

To see how arts liaison librarians are using visual arts to communicate with students and faculty, see stories by Megan Lotts and Jill Chisnell.

Arts-based Scholarship in Libraries

It's worth considering here how libraries have historically served as the repositories for traditional products of scholarship like books and journals. What does this mean for arts-based scholarship? Do such works belong with their more traditional counterparts? Consider that the countless ranges of printed matter found in every library are, in a very real sense, the reflection of the creative work of humanity, the creation and synthesis of ideas and meaning. Arts-based scholarship comes in these same physical forms, but also many others as well, all from the same lineage of human creativity. If we conclude that practice-based research in other forms does belong, are libraries prepared for custodial care that has often focused exclusively on printed matter and data?

For examples of arts liaison librarians modeling a way forward for libraries to embrace practice-based scholarship that includes creative art in library spaces, see stories by Courtney Hunt, Courtney McLeland and Tom Caswell, and Jenna Rinalducci.

Sometimes you'll find a particular avenue of engagement that meets a number of different needs for various communities. As the founder and curator of a large books arts collection at my institution, I (Sha) have created pop-up galleries and exhibits in various locations including the libraries, art department, and university art gallery. One public exhibit in particular was the culmination of a course in which I was embedded liaison, where I served as a consultant for the exhibit and was invited to write the preface to the exhibition catalog. While these events are open to the public, I often schedule them to align with relevant courses and collaborate with instructors to integrate these experiences into their classes. Often these events include public talks by artists and art dealers and comingle art history students learning about the medium and its context in art history with studio arts students who are exploring the collection as inspiration for their own artwork. This type of activity merges promoting special collections and the libraries, partnering with instructors, addressing different types of research, and extending the reach of engagement.

Figure 8.1. Collaborative Pop-Up Book Arts Fair, Baylor University

New Skill Sets for Arts Liaisons

Many arts liaisons have expanded their skill sets to include a variety of new technologies. Some of these are technologies that have risen to prominence during the COVID-19 pandemic, requiring liaisons to pivot quickly to new modes of research support, as well as new modes for learning and teaching, that require expertise in learning management systems, video conferencing tools, and video creation platforms. While some of these adaptations and resulting modalities may only last for a season of extenuating circumstances, others may become part of the new normal. Some liaisons are supporting their constituents with skills in digitizing and data management while others are serving as the conduit for such services between faculty and specialized technologists either elsewhere in the library or campus. It's important to note here that a particular technology may not be central to the actual research, but nonetheless it is crucial to the business of doing research.

A particular skill area relevant for those working as liaisons in the arts is visual literacy. While this type of literacy has implications in all fields, it is crucially important in visual arts and design disciplines. Visual literacy is often thought of as the ability to read images—to interpret and make meaning from nontextual information. Whether this is the understanding of what the icon commonly used to indicate radioactivity means or understanding mythological references in a painting from the Western Classical tradition, visual literacy is an area with which liaisons serving the arts should be familiar.[7]

One way in which visual literacy is explored and practiced for art students is by visiting art museums and exhibits; often arts liaisons can further connect with faculty and students by joining in these experiences. For examples of how art liaison librarians have embedded in this type of experience, see the stories by Shelley Woods and Jenna Dufour.

Digital Scholarship in the Arts

Another area of growing importance for the arts is in digital scholarship. We use this term as an umbrella for any of the pedagogies, approaches, and tools that help us see and understand data and information in new ways. Digital scholarship includes various domains such as data visualization, text data mining, geospatial analysis, and data management. While not unique to the arts, digital scholarship can significantly influence arts research in many ways. Here are just a few examples of how researchers might incorporate digital scholarship into their research:

- Mining the entire corpus of Shakespeare's plays for network analysis of previously unrecognized patterns
- Mapping the migration of Italian Renaissance composers to investigate international influences
- Analyzing the evolution of Van Gogh's color palette over his career[8]
- Visualizing contemporary dance through a movement analysis tool[9]

Digital scholarship also provides tools for practice-based scholarship as artists create new work. Examples of data-driven art include:

- Musical composition based on earthquake data[10]
- Sculpture based on weather data[11]
- Interactive visual art installation based on health sciences data[12]

The stories shared by arts liaisons reflect a wide scope of engagement with arts faculty and students and, in particular, illuminate a variety of ways to support creative practice in the arts. Some of these will have explicit connections to supporting research and others demonstrate more subtle, but no less important, connections through making, marketing, and establishing exhibition venues and even bringing subject matter expertise to the table.

For examples of art liaison librarians bringing discipline expertise into experiences with arts students and faculty and embedding in co-instructor opportunities, see stories by Scott Stone and Sha Towers.

PROFESSIONAL LIBRARY ASSOCIATIONS IN THE ARTS INCLUDE:

- Art Libraries Society of North America (ARLIS/NA): arlisna.org
- Music Library Association (MLA): musiclibraryassoc.org
- Theatre Library Association (TLA): tla-online.org
- Association of College and Research Libraries–Arts Section: (ACRLArts) acrl.ala.org/arts/

RELEVANT LIBRARY LISTSERVS AND DISCUSSION GROUPS IN THE ARTS INCLUDE:

- acrl-arts@lists.ala.org (ACRL–Arts Section Discussion List)
- listserv@lsv.arlisna.org (ARLIS/NA Listserv)
- mla-l-subscribe@indiana.edu (MLA Listserv)
- dance@lists.ala.org (ACRL Arts Dance Librarians Discussion Group)
- http://www.tla-online.org/news/tla-l-listserv/ (TLA Listserv)

◉ Stories of Engagement with the Arts

Stories can be read in the supplement at the publisher's website.
www.liaisonengagementsuccess.com

- Creative Collaboration: Research as Creative Act in the Art Studio Classroom—by Bria Sinnott, Towson University
    "This was not a planned partnership; it came from a place of organic inquiry, informed by observation and collegial conversation. By anchoring the session in studio practices, students were able to consider research as part *of*—not apart *from*—their creative process."
- Providing Library Outreach to Artists—by Nimisha Bhat, Smith College
    "The information-seeking behaviors of art students often vary widely, as they require a great deal of information that often has no epistemic relationship to art. Studio art students are among the most difficult to bring into the library since they often perceive libraries and library research as irrelevant to and incompatible with their art production. This made me wonder how to create a viable library reference model for art students at my institution."
- Dramaturgy in Action: Research Out to the Stage—by Scott Stone, University of California, Irvine
    "Generally, the dramaturg presents information to and answers questions from the entire cast and artistic crew so that they can best understand the new play world they're creating and any social issues that are being explored thematically in the play. These activities certainly sound similar to what a typical liaison librarian might do when working with their users, so it was just a short stretch for me to move into dramaturging some of the main stage play production at the University of California, Irvine (UCI)."

Figure 8.2. Stone with the cast and crew of UCI's production of Lisa Loomer's play *Living Out* during a show talk in February 2020

- Creating Artists' Statements—by Andi Back, University of Kansas

    "During these conversations the librarian introduces resources that assist all of the students in their writing and how to situate their own work among the larger art world and beyond. Examples of resources include collections of artists' writings, writings about artists' work, guides on how to write about art, vocational guidance, trade journals, and books about particular artists or topics relevant to the work of the particular students in the course. By allowing the librarian to engage in these discussions, the students recognize librarians themselves as resources."

- The Art Library Coloring Book—by Megan Lotts, Rutgers University

    "[T]his project was created as a learning resource to bring new users to the Art Library. In addition, it provides an alternative way for a library liaison to connect with users who might not understand how an artist engages with a library when writing about or making art."

- Librarian Makes a Zine—by Jill Chisnell, Carnegie Mellon University

    "In fall 2019, rather than send a boring blanket departmental email to welcome the start of the new academic year, I created a zine for design faculty and instructors. *Date Due: The Library Zine* is 'a little bit newsletter about the University Libraries and a whole lotta love letter to libraries.'"

- Embedded in Game Design—by Shelley Woods, Sheridan College

    "I've been told, on numerous occasions, that I have a cool job. I'm the Liaison Librarian for Animation, Arts and Design at Sheridan College. I get this reaction after describing a Virtual Merchandising Arts field trip to New York City, a design conference in Chicago, Ubisoft Faculty Night, a talk by Disney, a researcher credit in the IMDB movie database, and building material, game, and zine library collections among other events and projects."

Figure 8.3. Jill Chisnell's *Date Due: The Library Zine*

- Liaison Engagement through Art and Museum Visits—by Jenna Dufour, University of California, Irvine

    "This informal engagement also helped shift some of the power dynamics that result in a traditional workshop setting. Since some of the students got to know me outside of the formal classroom/library environment first, I wasn't just a 'Professional Librarian With Answers' but a lifelong learner, new to these artists as well, and generally just a friendly and approachable human."

- Exhibiting Student Artwork in the Fine Arts Library—by Courtney Hunt, The Ohio State University

    "Outreach and engagement were the main priorities for my first year at OSU and still are. With this in mind, I decided to start showing student artwork in the library in the Fall of 2019."

- Building Together: A Dedicated Space for Student Art Exhibits—by Courtenay McLeland and Tom Caswell, University of North Florida

  "Although student artwork had been displayed in the library previously through the efforts of the library exhibits committee, there had been a strong desire by the art liaisons and others to establish a more permanent and dedicated area for the exhibition of artwork by students."

- Fragments from the Library of Babel: A Student Mural Collaboration—by Jenna Rinalducci, University of North Carolina at Charlotte

  "Ultimately, the final project unified the scholarship of both fine arts and architecture students in their shared college. It also provided students with real-world applications of their scholarship, with the library acting as client and the student as provider."

- The Liaison Librarian as Artist—by Sha Towers, Baylor University

  "If you are a liaison librarian with background in arts disciplines or who happens to be a practicing artist, this may open doors for deeper levels of involvement with your constituents. Practicing your art alongside other artists is not only rewarding and enriching for the librarian, but lays the groundwork for deep and meaningful connections and conveys your interest and support for the things that matter to your constituents."

Key Points

- Don't expect all research and scholarship in the arts to look the same.
- Creative modalities are an important aspect of research and scholarship in the arts.
- Familiarize yourself with the domains, and distinctions between them, of arts-based research and research-based art.
- Take advantage of professional organizations in the arts and the resources for librarians in these disciplines specifically.

Notes

1. Ian Chilvers, ed., "Fine Arts," in *The Oxford Dictionary of Art and Artists*, Oxford Reference Online (Oxford: University Press, 2015); Michael Kelly, ed., "Decorative Arts," in *Encyclopedia of Aesthetics*, Oxford Reference Online (New York: Oxford University Press, 2014).

2. Linda Candy and Ernest Edmonds, "Practice-Based Research in the Creative Arts: Foundations and Futures from the Front Line," *Leonardo (Oxford)* 51, no. 1 (2018): 63–69, https://doi.org/10.1162/LEON_a_01471.

3. Monica Pentassuglia, "'The Art(Ist) Is Present': Arts-Based Research Perspective in Educational Research," *Cogent Education* 4, no. 1 (2017), https://doi.org/10.1080/2331186x.2017.1301011.

4. Tom Barone and Elliot W. Eisner, *Arts Based Research*, 1st ed. (Los Angeles: Sage, 2011), 7.

5. Barone and Eisner, *Arts Based Research*, 8–9.

6. "2019 Altmetric Research Grant Winners to Investigate Altmetrics for Creative and Performing Arts Research," *Altmetric* (blog), June 26, 2019, https://www.altmetric.com/press/press-releases/2019-grant-arts-research/.

7. For more on visual literacy, see https://visualliteracytoday.org; James Elkins, ed., *Visual Literacy*, 1st ed. (New York: Routledge, 2007); Frank Serafini, *Reading the Visual: An Introduction to Teaching Multimodal Literacy* (New York: Teachers College Press, 2013).

8. Jason Bailey, "New Data Shows Why Van Gogh Changed His Color Palette," *Artnome*, December 24, 2018, https://www.artnome.com/news/2018/11/26/new-data-shows-why-van -gogh-changed-his-color-palette-to-bright-yellow.

9. K. Carlson, T. Schiphorst, and C. Shaw, "ActionPlot: A Visualization Tool for Contemporary Dance Analysis," in *Proceedings of the International Symposium on Computational Aesthetics in Graphics, Visualization, and Imaging—CAe '11* (the International Symposium, Vancouver, British Columbia, Canada: ACM Press, 2011), 113, https://doi.org/10.1145/2030441.2030466.

10. Adrienne Steely, "'Cycles' for Full Orchestra and Electronics" (Thesis, Waco, TX, Baylor University, 2016), https://baylor-ir.tdl.org/handle/2104/9915.

11. Nathalie Miebach, *Art Made of Storms*, TEDGlobal 2011, 2011, https://www.ted.com /talks/nathalie_miebach_art_made_of_storms.

12. Julia Hitchcock, "A Contemporary Altarpiece for Our Techno-Human Age," Department of Art and Art History at Baylor University, October 25, 2016, https://www.baylor.edu/art/news .php?action=story&story=177189.

CHAPTER 9

Engagement with the Professional Disciplines

⑥ What Are the Professional Disciplines?

A *PROFESSION* CAN BE DEFINED AS AN "occupational group characterized by: the use of skills based on theoretical knowledge; prolonged education and training; professional competence ensured by examinations; a code of conduct; the performance of a service which is for the public good; and a professional association that organizes its members."[1] Traditionally, the earliest professions were the church, the military, law, and medicine. However, as society has developed, what once were trades became formalized; tradespeople became organized, created schools to train people with codified skills, and began to guard the boundaries of the profession through licensures and codes of ethics.

Being a liaison to a professional discipline may come easily to an academic librarian, as they themselves have been formed by a professional discipline through the process of obtaining a master's of library science degree. In addition, some academic liaison librarians are on the tenure track, and so have the same research and publishing requirements as the faculty in their liaison departments.

TRADITIONAL PROFESSIONAL DISCIPLINES

- Education (can also be considered a social science discipline)
  - Curriculum and instruction
  - Educational administration
  - Educational psychology
  - Educational technology
- Business (can also be considered a social science discipline)
  - Management
  - Marketing
  - Accounting
  - Finance
  - Information systems
- Library and information science
- Law (can also be considered a humanities discipline)
- Social work
- Criminal justice
- Public administration
- Urban planning
- Health occupations (can also be considered STEM disciplines)
  - Medicine
  - Veterinary medicine
  - Dentistry
  - Pharmacy
  - Nursing
  - Physical therapy
  - Occupational therapy
  - Communication sciences and disorders
  - Nutrition
  - Clinical psychology
  - Public health
- Journalism
- Fine arts (can be considered an arts discipline)
- Theater (can be considered an arts discipline)
- Film and media (can be considered an arts discipline)
- Design occupations (can be considered an arts discipline)
  - Interior design
  - Fashion design
  - Graphic design
- Architecture (can be considered an arts discipline)
  - Interior
  - Landscape
- Engineering (can be considered a STEM discipline)
  - Chemical
  - Civil
  - Electrical
  - Material science
  - Mechanical

Faculty members in professional disciplines who research may find themselves caught in a tension between research in a "pure" discipline versus research in an "applied" or professional discipline, which is research concerned with the practical nature, usefulness, and application of the knowledge acquired. The conversation around issues in a professional discipline can often include professional practitioners, who may not publish in scholarly journals, even if they publish at all. *Applied research* is defined by the object of study, for example, higher education, librarianship, or business management, and therefore the method of the research may come from a variety of disciplines.[2] Therefore, professional researchers may need to read widely from a variety of fields. Their liaisons, who are often aware of resources and tools in a wide variety of disciplines, and are adept at tracking down and accessing other types of information, including from nonscholarly sources, are vital to helping professional researchers stay aware of and keep up with multiple information streams.

Clinical Faculty and Practical Skills

In professional disciplines, you may find faculty with a different title: that of "Clinical Professor" or "Professor of Practice." These faculty are qualified because of their practical knowledge and their experience in their professional discipline. While some may engage in research, a teaching agenda focused on practical skills rather than theoretical knowledge is more common. They may also supervise the students in a clinical, internship, or practicum program as a part of their duties. While the name *clinical* comes from the health field, in which a professor may teach at a medical or health sciences university while also working in a clinic, you can find clinical professors in social work, education, business, law, or engineering.

To understand how some liaisons have connected their services to service learning and practical field experiences, see the stories of Michelle Shea and Terry Henner.

Professional Identity

Developing a professional identity, where students become nurses, accountants, teachers, or social workers, among others, is a formative part of any educational program in a professional discipline. This process socializes students to identify with professional norms, helps them understand professional discourse, and allows them to recognize the power of the profession to regulate both who enters the profession and how a professional practices their job.

Professional disciplines are often committed to a code of ethics, set by their professional organizations or associations. These codes govern their interactions with the public and protect the reputation of the profession as a whole. For example, liaison librarians will be aware of the American Library Association Code of Ethics, which states, in part,

"We protect each library user's right to privacy and confidentiality with respect to information sought or received and resources consulted, borrowed, acquired or transmitted."[3] This particular statement guides librarians to guard a patron's records and to not publicly broadcast what question a particular patron may have asked at the reference desk. Other professions have similar codes.

Even though it may be difficult for a liaison to understand a discipline's professional identity from the outside, it is not impossible. Enrolling in or auditing classes can help, as can attending conferences put on by professional associations. Just reading through professional association documents (mission, vision, code of ethics) can be of help.

To experience how a liaison sought to understand the discipline she served, see the story of Sarah Nicholas. To find out how another liaison positioned herself as a professional expert, see the story of Afra Bolefski.

Continuing Education

One way in which professional disciplines guard the boundaries of their profession is through licensure and continuing education (CE). Training students to a particular standard to gain a license to work in the profession and then requiring CE credits on a regular basis is an important part of medical professions as well as education, social work, engineering, and a wide variety of business and design professions. Librarians can sometimes be called upon—or can volunteer their services—to help provide CE courses for credit.

To read about how some liaisons have become instructors for their professional student populations, see the stories of Michael Saar and Karen S. Alcorn.

Student Population

Be aware of whether the professional programs you support as a liaison are made up of full-time students or people taking classes alongside working a full-time job. Knowing the kinds of student learners you are supporting may help you figure out the kinds of services you should provide, particularly when it comes to setting hours. Perhaps you need to offer your appointment hours or workshops in the evening or weekend hours. As the main Zotero trainer for our campus, I (Ellen) am often called upon to provide these workshops on the weekend or in the evenings to our EdD programs, as the majority of the students work full-time jobs outside the program. Learning how your user communities operate (see chapter 2) can help you tailor your services to their needs.

To appreciate the full picture of a medical school liaison librarian, see the story of Marisol Hernandez.

RELEVANT LIBRARY LISTSERVS IN THE PROFESSIONAL DISCIPLINES

- liscdg-l@lists.ala.org (Association of College and Research Libraries [ACRL] Library and Information Science Collections Discussion Group)
- ebss-l@lists.ala.org (ACRL Education and Behavioral Sciences Section)
- brass-l@lists.ala.org (BRASS-L provides all Business Reference and Services Section (BRASS) members news and information about the Reference and User Services Association–BRASS programs and activities.)
- medref@lists.ala.org (Reference Services Section Health and Medical Reference)
- acrl-hsig@lists.purdue.edu (Health Sciences Interest Group of ACRL)

Stories of Engagement in the Professions

Stories can be read in the supplement at the publisher's website.
www.liaisonengagementsuccess.com

- Inhabiting a Professional World—by Sarah Nicholas, Cardiff University
    "I wanted the impetus for my approach to engagement to come from within the discipline, rather than the discipline being the context in which I operated. I didn't want to be the information professional didactically imposing her notion of what was best for the school. This paradigm shift in my approach to liaison work was, I felt, essential."
- Becoming the Bloomberg Expert—by Afra Bolefski, University of Manitoba
    "In this story, I would like to share my liaison experience of how I was able to get a foothold into the Finance department by taking on the unique role of resident Bloomberg expert."
- Engaging Education Students in Tutoring and Service Learning—by Michelle Shea, Texas A&M University–Central Texas
    "The library is pleased to provide liaison services that allow for applied learning, alongside our more conventional research help."
- Predatory Journal Continuing Education Credit—by Michael Saar, Lamar University
    "The presentation lasted a mere hour although the direct preparation occurred over several months. Yet the genesis of this project was the result of several years of relationship building that required patience and capitalizing on opportunities."

Figure 9.1. Architecture undergraduates sketching next to the River Liffey in Dublin. *Photo credit: Sarah Nicholas*

- Embedded in the Life of a Medical School—by Marisol Hernandez, City University of New York School of Medicine

  "My specific work with the medical students involves training and consultation on literature searching skills, product navigation, systematic review methodology, and scholarly communication."

- Liaisons Connecting to Community Telehealth Practitioners—by Terry Henner, University of Nevada, Reno

  "One foundational aspect of health outreach is the establishment of liaison roles that create linkages between librarians and those practitioners whose work takes place outside of traditional academic settings. This brief case study outlines how an academic health sciences library established a liaison service role to support a telehealth/telementoring outreach program known as Project ECHO Nevada."

- Teaching Evidence-Based Practice in Physical Therapy—by Karen S. Alcorn, Massachusetts College of Pharmacy and Health Sciences University

  "My hope is this instruction allows my students to excel in their profession, preparing them to use EBP to provide the best care to their patients, as well as contributing to the improvement of physical therapy practice."

Key Points

- Professional disciplines can feel the tension between the "academic" and the "practical/professional" sides of their teaching and research.
- Liaisons to professional disciplines should consider the role of the "clinical professor" and how they function in their user communities.

- Codes of ethics and continuing education credits are ways in which professional boundaries and standards are maintained.
- Nontraditional students or students working full-time jobs can make up professional programs, so nontraditional services may need to be offered.

Notes

1. Kenneth McLeish, ed., "Profession," in *Bloomsbury Guide to Human Thought* (Bloomsbury, 1993).

2. Sarah Rose Fitzgerald, "Serving a Fragmented Field: Information Seeking in Higher Education," *The Journal of Academic Librarianship* 44, no. 3 (May 1, 2018): 337–42, https://doi.org/10.1016/j.acalib.2018.03.007.

3. American Library Association, "Professional Ethics," Text, Tools, Publications and Resources, May 19, 2017, http://www.ala.org/tools/ethics.

Engagement with Nonacademic Units

Extending Liaison Relationships to Nonacademic Departments

IN A 2007 ARTICLE, CANDACE DAHL SUGGESTED that the model of the liaison librarian be extended to include liaison relationships with nonacademic departments on college and university campuses.[1] Since that article, many libraries have created both formal and informal partnerships in these areas. Formal partnerships include creating positions that are specifically dedicated to liaison work with these units, whether they are called *liaisons* or not, and informal partnerships that refer to one-off or recurring programs in collaboration with these units. While there are some librarians in positions who work specifically with nonacademic units on campus and are called *liaisons*, many other positions have different names: *student success librarian, outreach librarian, first-year experience librarian, undergraduate engagement librarian,* and *undergraduate services librarian* among many others.[2] Regardless of whether a library position aimed at working with nonacademic units is officially called a *liaison* or not, or even whether it is located organizationally within a liaison unit in the library, the point that Dahl emphasized in her article is that the skills and methods that liaisons have built in their work with academic units—the outreach, relationship-building, listening, communication, and collaboration skills—are needed in this work with nonacademic units. She states:

By extending the liaison model to include nonacademic units the library gains both partners and an increased presence on campus. Both libraries and these nonacademic units will benefit from the formalized relationship that the liaison model offers, especially at a time when integrated services and shared spaces are increasingly present on university campuses. . . . By applying the principles of established liaison programs to nonacademic units, libraries can position themselves to engage in more systematic and inclusive liaison initiatives on their campuses.[3]

The Association of College and Research Libraries' (ACRL) "Value of Academic Libraries" initiative has set forth priorities for demonstrating how academic libraries provide value to and advance the missions of their institutions. They suggest doing so by having librarians "establish, assess, and link academic library outcomes to institutional outcomes related to the following areas: student enrollment, student retention and graduation rates, student success, student achievement, student learning, [and] student engagement."[4] These are all areas of student affairs departments on university campuses that don't typically, without purposeful effort, interact with the library. Being able to establish a formal connection to this part of campus can be a good first step toward working together to advance institutional priorities.

There has been a movement over the last few decades to create partnerships with nonacademic units by co-locating similar services within the library building, through spaces that have often been called Learning or Information Commons. These areas within libraries are often visible and accessible, and they seek to bring any number of student services from across campus, alongside library and information technology assistance.[5] While the physical proximity these spaces provide might be able to bring about some spontaneous shared programming ideas, without personnel dedicated to that strategic effort, it can often get relegated to a lower priority.

However, being able to create a new position dedicated to this type of campus engagement can be difficult, particularly in an era of budget freezes or cutbacks. It's equally difficult to find someone to take on this work if current liaison librarians have overloaded portfolios. Because of these challenges, some libraries have found creative ways to accomplish this work. At Baylor University, a team of liaison librarians have taken it upon themselves to engage with just a few strategic student success programs, like the McNair Scholars or New Student Experience programs. At the University of North Alabama, the library established a program in which the library staff became liaisons to campus departments, becoming a valued channel of communication both to and from the library.

To learn how one library established a program in which the library staff became liaisons to campus departments, see the story by Derek Malone.

POSSIBLE NONACADEMIC UNITS FOR LIAISON ASSIGNMENTS

- Student affairs
  - Advising
  - Student support
  - Tutoring
  - Learning accommodation
  - Career services
  - First-generation student services
  - First-year experience
- Administrative
  - Admissions
  - Enrollment
  - Financial aid
- Campus life
  - Student activities
  - Greek life
  - Veterans services
  - Athletics
  - Student government
  - LGBTQ support services
  - International student services
  - Chaplain services
- Residence life
  - Living-learning communities
- Departments that are not academic disciplines, but have an academic focus
  - Center for Teaching and Learning
  - Service learning
  - Writing center
  - Study abroad
  - Graduate student office

How to Engage with Nonacademic Departments

If you are a liaison to a nonacademic area, whether it is a full-time position or extra duties added to your liaison portfolio, you should keep these important things in mind. First, build relationships just like a regular subject liaison. Get to know the key people in whatever administrative department you are partnering with. Who are the main administrators? Who oversees programming for the department? Who are the leaders who get things done? You won't know who is ripe for collaboration until you put in the time building relationships.

Relationship building was paramount for one librarian at the University of Oklahoma, who was able to live in the dorms for several years as a faculty in residence.[6] While there, she built relationships with resident assistants and residential life staff and provided programming that was in line with the educational mission of the residence hall that often had a library or information literacy aspect to it. Even after moving out of the dorms, she continued her outreach to the residence halls, using the strategies she had honed during her years living in residence: find the right space, match the libraries' goals with the goals of the residential life office, and find the right people who are in the position to collaborate.

One librarian, who is also a military veteran, was able to build relationships with the veteran community at Texas A&M University. Because of these relationships, the Texas A&M libraries have designed an orientation program for the university's large veteran population modeled after the common military method for orientation called an "in-processing checklist." The library team that designed the service drew from military culture to provide a culturally relevant way to deliver the information that this population needed.[7]

To discover how another liaison built relationships with students in a residence hall, see the story by Kristina Clement.

Ask Good Questions

When developing relationships, ask good questions about the work that they are doing. What goals are they pursuing with their work? What aspects of the university's mission are their focus? Do they provide services for the students' academic, personal, mental, physical, or emotional needs? When during the students' time at the university do students cross paths with their office? Where are they succeeding and where are they finding points of pain? What are the students they come in contact with most interested in? Asking question of these potential partners can function the same way as a traditional reference interview, during which you are listening to find out the needs of the students served by these departments. Just as you wouldn't answer a student question about COVID-19 without finding out whether they have a need for scholarly information or a list of symptoms, you shouldn't just respond to all student needs with an information literacy session.[8] The University of Oklahoma faculty-in-residence librarian summed up the importance of asking good questions, but also listening to their answers: "[O]utreach success awaits the librarian who is willing to take that literal first step over the threshold, to observe and explore, and, most importantly, to listen to the students and staff."[9]

Find the Connections

As you build relationships with units across campus and learn about the work that they are doing, find the connections between their department's mission and goals and the library's. The overlap in mission is where the most successful programming will happen, because both partners will be invested in its success. Partnering to put on events or to provide information or services eases the workload, can help stretch any budgets that are available, can use multiple channels for promotion, and demonstrates intrainstitutional collaboration to higher-up administrators.[10]

One example of how liaisons might find connections is through looking at the types of partnerships libraries have had with the offices of Greek Life or Athletics, which may seem at first glance to have very different missions than the departments of the academic side of the university. However, these offices often maintain academic standards for their students, like a certain grade point average, to participate. In the case of athletics, these standards are set by the NCAA. Understanding those priorities have led libraries to partner with these groups to provide services, including tours, orientations, and tailored instructional sessions, as a way to promote academic success among these tight-knit campus groups.[11]

Collaborating with student support services offices on campus can be very fruitful. Student affairs administrators will be aware of the higher education research that asserts that student engagement has positive effects on retention and persistence rates,[12] so getting students involved in extra- or cocurricular activities is a high priority. The libraries make a natural partner.[13] In addition, the 2010 ACRL report "Value of Academic Libraries" stated that libraries can demonstrate their value to the university by collaborating with student affairs professionals and libraries to contribute to retention and enrollment goals,[14] which can be a strong incentive for this type of partnership.

To learn about the partnership between a liaison and the staff and peer mentors of the campus writing center, see the story by Erin Durham, Zoe Hwang, and Elaine MacDougall (also referred to in chapter 11). To read about how a liaison teamed up with the career services department to serve their community, see the story by Sandra Shoufani.

Assess Collaboratively

As you put on any programming or events, or create new services at the library, make sure to assess them, and do so in collaboration with your campus partners. Without assessment, you won't know whether to continue the program or service, change aspects of it, or cancel it.[15] Different departments have different ways of doing assessment, of course, but surveys, anecdotal responses, and statistics can be easily gathered and provide good feedback.[16]

Having a partnership with another department on campus means that it is vital to have systems in place for referrals. That way, when students come to the library and indicate that they have a need for something that is provided by that other department or vice versa—the student lets the staff in that department know of their need for information that the library provides—students can easily be referred to the right place. Perhaps you have students coming to the library looking for accessible textbooks, but because of a partnership with the office of learning accommodations, you are now aware that they can find services through that office, so you can refer them to the right place—or even to the right person.

Whether your full-time job is an outreach position focused on student services, or you have dabbled in a project or partnership once in a while during your career, engaging with nonacademic units of the university can be very rewarding, both for the library and the staff of the partnering department. Ultimately, the goal of this engagement is to serve students while furthering the goals and mission of the university.

To consider how some liaisons have partnered with graduate studies offices to serve the graduate population in both social and academic ways, see the stories by Amy Dye-Reeves and by Roxanne Bogucka and Meryl Brodsky.

RELEVANT LIBRARY LISTSERVS FOR ENGAGEMENT ON CAMPUS:

- acr-iglmo@lists.ala.org (ACRL Library Marketing and Outreach Interest Group)
- acrl-fye@lists.ala.org (ACRL First-Year Experience Discussion Group)

Stories of Engagement with Nonacademic Units

Stories can be read in the supplement at the publisher's website.
www.liaisonengagementsuccess.com

- Liaising Where They Live: Hosting Library Office Hours at the First-Generation Student Dorm—by Kristina Clement, University of Wyoming
    "The University of Wyoming wanted to make Tobin House a dynamic learning community of approximately sixty first-generation freshmen and several Junior and Senior resident assistants, and they were thrilled that the library wanted to have a presence in the house."
- Teaming up with Career Services to Serve the Local Community—by Sandra Shoufani, Sheridan College
    "The positives of this initiative are many, including sharing Sheridan's specialized career readiness knowledge with the general public, building a mutually beneficial library-to-library community partnership, and creating a fruitful interdepartment collaboration between a librarian and an employment consultant."
- Creating a Library Staff Liaison Program to Nonacademic Departments—by Derek Malone, University of North Alabama
    "Therefore, starting in the spring 2020 semester, staff from Collier Library and Information Services began liaison activities with nonacademic departments, such as Athletics, Human Resources, the Diversity and Institutional Equity office, the Career Center, Alumni Relations, Housing and Residential Life, and Student Affairs, among others. The outcome has been tremendous."
- Creating a Doctoral Support Center—by Amy Dye-Reeves, Texas Tech University
    "The purpose of the committee was to look at the various stages and life cycles of a doctoral student—the progression of the student, including prospective, first, second, third, and beyond."

- Collaborating with the Office of Graduate Studies for a Graduate Research Showcase—by Roxanne Bogucka and Meryl Brodsky

  "It may have given some graduate students and faculty who would not otherwise have encountered each other an opportunity to meet, opening pathways for interdisciplinary collaboration and research. The collaboration with the Office of Graduate Studies will help to keep the Libraries top of mind when OGS seeks partners for future events."

Figure 10.1. Graduate Research Showcase student presenter Kolina Koltai. *Photo credit: Roxanne Bogucka*

Key points

- Nonacademic departments in a college or university setting are fertile ground for liaison work.
- Whether this liaison relationship is your full-time job, or extra duties, treat it how you would any liaison work: build relationships first.
- After building relationships, then listen, figure out shared goals, and collaborate on events, services, and assessment.

Notes

1. Candice C. Dahl, "Library Liaison with Non-Academic Units: A New Application for a Traditional Model," *Partnership: The Canadian Journal of Library and Information Practice and Research* 2, no. 1 (May 21, 2007), https://doi.org/10.21083/partnership.v2i1.242.

2. Lily Todorinova, "A Mixed-Method Study of Undergraduate and First Year Librarian Positions in Academic Libraries in the United States," *The Journal of Academic Librarianship* 44, no. 2 (March 1, 2018): 207–15, https://doi.org/10.1016/j.acalib.2018.02.005.

3. Dahl, "Library Liaison with Non-Academic Units," 8.

4. Megan Oakleaf, "The Value of Academic Libraries: A Comprehensive Research Review and Report" (Chicago: Association of College and Research Libraries, American Library Association, 2010), 12.

5. Amy Wainwright and Chris Davidson, "Academic Libraries and Non-Academic Departments: A Survey and Case Studies on Liaising Outside the Box," *Collaborative Librarianship* 9, no. 2 (2017): 19.

6. Molly Strothmann and Karen Antell, "The Live-In Librarian: Developing Library Outreach to University Residence Halls," *Reference and User Services Quarterly* 50, no. 1 (2010): 48–58.

7. Sarah LeMire et al., "Basic Training: A Library Orientation Designed for Student Veterans," *The Journal of Academic Librarianship* 46, no. 4 (July 1, 2020): 102137, https://doi.org/10.1016/j.acalib.2020.102137.

8. Tammi M. Owens and Katie Bishop, "'Let's Try It!': Library Outreach in a Culture of Yes," *Public Services Quarterly* 14, no. 1 (February 14, 2018): 75–82, https://doi.org/10.1080/15228959.2017.1411861.

9. Strothmann and Antell, "The Live-In Librarian," 57.

10. Pauline S. Swartz, Brian A. Carlisle, and E. Chisato Uyeki, "Libraries and Student Affairs: Partners for Student Success," *Reference Services Review* 35, no. 1 (January 1, 2007): 109–22, https://doi.org/10.1108/00907320710729409; Erin E. Meyer, "Low-Hanging Fruit: Leveraging Short-Term Partnerships to Advance Academic Library Outreach Goals," *Collaborative Librarianship* 6, no. 3 (2014): 10; Emily Love, "Building Bridges: Cultivating Partnerships between Libraries and Minority Student Services," *Education Libraries* 30, no. 1 (September 5, 2017): 13, https://doi.org/10.26443/el.v30i1.232.

11. A. Blake Denton, "Academic Library and Athletics Partnerships: A Literature Review on Outreach Strategies and Development Opportunities," *The Southeastern Librarian* 67, no. 2 (2019): 8; Lynn D. Lampert, Katherine S. Dabbour, and Jacqueline Solis, "When It's All Greek: The Importance of Collaborative Information Literacy Outreach Programming to Greek Student Organizations," *Research Strategies* 20, no. 4 (January 1, 2005): 300–310, https://doi.org/10.1016/j.resstr.2006.12.005.

12. George D. Kuh et al., "Unmasking the Effects of Student Engagement on First-Year College Grades and Persistence," *The Journal of Higher Education* 79, no. 5 (September 2008): 540–63, https://doi.org/10.1080/00221546.2008.11772116.

13. Swartz, Carlisle, and Chisato Uyeki, "Libraries and Student Affairs"; Kathryn Crowe, "Student Affairs Connection: Promoting the Library through Co-Curricular Activities," *Collaborative Librarianship* 2, no. 3 (2010): 154–58, https://doi.org/10.29087/2010.2.3.02; Wainwright and Davidson, "Academic Libraries and Non-Academic Departments"; Emily Love and Margaret B. Edwards, "Forging Inroads between Libraries and Academic, Multicultural and Student Services," *Reference Services Review* 37, no. 1 (January 1, 2009): 20–29, https://doi.org/10.1108/00907320910934968.

14. Oakleaf, "The Value of Academic Libraries."

15. Love, "Building Bridges."

16. Love and Edwards, "Forging Inroads between Libraries and Academic, Multicultural and Student Services."

CHAPTER 11

Collaboration and Partnership Inside and Outside the Library

IN THIS CHAPTER

▷ Partnering with other liaisons

▷ Partnering with functional specialists

   ○ Digital scholarship
   ○ Scholarly communication
   ○ Special collections
   ○ Information literacy and instruction

▷ Partnering with technology specialists

   ○ Learning spaces
   ○ Makerspaces
   ○ Media spaces

▷ Stories of collaboration and partnership

◎ Partnering with Other Liaisons

UNLESS YOU'RE THE ONLY LIAISON LIBRARIAN at your institution, chances are you're already partnering with your colleagues on some level. Perhaps your institution is the size that has clusters of liaisons for STEM, humanities, or social sciences. Maybe there is only one liaison for the sciences and another for business and you don't have subject "birds of a feather." Whatever your circumstance, we recommend that you look for any common ground you can find for moral support and to share strengths and strategies with one another. If you're fortunate enough to have a team of liaisons at your institution, you have the added benefit of partnering with colleagues to provide interdisciplinary support to your researchers, faculty, and students. While it's sometimes necessary to go it alone as a liaison, if you have the opportunity to leverage the disciplinary strengths of your colleagues, they can provide stronger and more diverse support to your clients and can be a rewarding experience for you as well. Often, the subject specializations among liaisons are not limited to discipline assignments. Maybe someone on your team is the resident expert in a particular citation tool, suite of databases, or systematic reviews. There will be times when you have to partner with colleagues outside of your liaison team, but don't overlook the resources in your own departmental neighborhood.

In the sections that follow, we'll discuss a variety of other kinds of partners for collaboration. Depending on your institution, these may be in your own department, other departments in the library, or other divisions or departments in your institution. In some cases, you may look to colleagues even beyond the bounds of your institution. The point, however, is not so much how your institution is organized, but rather to leave no stone unturned as you identify and explore people and resources that can enrich your own work and the services you provide to your constituents. We mentioned early not to overlook partnerships in your immediate area, but we would also add not to overlook collaboration opportunities with those in other parts of the library or institution.

⑥ Partnering with Functional Specialists

For the sake of this chapter, we will discuss specialists in two camps: functional specialists and technology specialists. It's not important what terms you use in your institution, nor is it important to quibble about whether a specialization is functional or technological or both. While these terms appear in library settings, they can be somewhat interchangeable or not used at all, so don't get hung up on this. The main goal here is to highlight examples of specialists who may be helpful to you whether they exist in your liaison department or not.

Regardless of what kind of collaborative partner, get to know these people and learn about their skills and interests. This is a great way to be more informed, but also to lay the groundwork for potential partnerships. Remember not to approach these conversations transactionally—that is, "What can I get out of this?"—but allow the conversation to reveal ways in which each of you could be helpful to the other. If you're unsure how to strike up a conversation with someone you don't already work with regularly, consider a few examples:

- "One of the faculty members I work with mentioned something I thought might be of interest to you."
- "Since you're an expert in X, could you offer me some ideas or tips on how I could incorporate that in my work with researchers?"
- "Would you be willing to join me on a meeting with a faculty member to talk about X? I think your expertise in that area would really be beneficial to the conversation."

You'll find several stories shared by contributors at the end of this chapter about possibilities for partnering with functional specialists.

Digital Scholarship

Digital scholarship is a term that will have different meanings in different settings. It may include tools and strategies in data visualization, data management, text and data mining, geospatial analysis, or scripting and programming. It may also include support and management of data repositories and open-access publishing. Maybe your institution has someone in charge of all of these areas or maybe you have a more distributed model. Some institutional models include liaisons working with dedicated specialists over many or most of these areas while others expect liaisons to develop skills in particular areas. Whatever your situation, find out who your local experts are and strike up a conversation. Maybe they are happy to work alongside you and your constituents, or maybe they are happy to teach you what they know or point you in the right direction. Perhaps you can convince them to offer workshops for liaisons in specific skill areas if they're not already doing this. At our institution, the director of data and digital scholarship resides in the research and engagement department (with our liaisons, special collections, and public services teams). While the director doesn't have liaison assignments, he works collaboratively with all of our liaisons as they meet with researchers and instructors and has developed and facilitated many successful projects working with liaisons and their clients. Additionally, he has also developed highly successful educational programs benefitting liaisons, faculty, and students. The first is a series of virtual, self-paced workshops available to any campus affiliates. Each workshop functions independently resulting in digital badges but participants may also combine them toward certification as a Data Scholar. The second program is the Data Research Fellowship, available to graduate students in any discipline, and faculty members in humanities disciplines for an intensive, funded summer fellowship.[1] Another opportunity specifically for partnering liaisons with specialized expertise in digital scholarship is in a new program called "Data Viz of the Week," which highlights micro projects between liaisons and the director of data and digital scholarship to identify datasets and visualize aspects of the data.[2] Hopefully these experiences will offer you some ideas to consider and explore in your own workplace.

Figure 11.1.   Dr. Heidi Hornik's art history course partnering with data and digital scholarship director Joshua Been for a student project to collect data, create metadata, and a visualization, Baylor University

Scholarly Communication

The Association of College and Research Libraries has defined *scholarly communication* as the "system through which research and other scholarly writings are created, evaluated for quality, disseminated to the scholarly community, and preserved for future use."[3] While librarians have always supported early stages of research, including searching for and identifying information, liaisons today are often active throughout the entire research cycle, including work with aspects of author rights, copyright, access requirements for grant-funded research, and open-access publishing. As noted previously, some institutions will include this type of work under the umbrella of digital scholarship. Even if you are already involved in these areas, be sure to seek out others in your library, institution, or professional circles and take advantage of what they have to offer, increasing your own skills, knowledge, and ability to support your constituents. In an arena like scholarly communication, it's important not to approach this as all or nothing; you don't have to be an expert in every single aspect of scholarly communication, nor should you necessarily expect to find in others an expertise in all aspects. If you're fortunate enough to have a scholarly communication librarian on your team or in your library, have conversations with them to better understand how the two of you can work together and how your partnerships can most effectively benefit your clients.

As with any of these areas of specialization, if your institution doesn't have a person or team established to focus on this content, maybe your first step is to start having conversations about it with your colleagues. Whether you do this as informal conversations or maybe a lunch discussion group, this could be a way to assess the situation and find out if anyone is currently working in that area. It could be a way to share ideas or make a more formal proposal for addressing gaps in knowledge or service. Ideas for exploration might include relevant webinars or reading. No matter what your situation, partnering with others will often provide greater service to your constituents.

Special Collections

Special collections provide a rich set of resources for the researchers, faculty, and students whom you support. Because of this, it's important to get to know colleagues in special collections, rare books and manuscripts, and archives and become familiar with their work and the wealth of materials they curate and preserve. These people can be strong allies and developing relationships with them can be an important symbiotic opportunity. Drawing on their expertise and materials can be beneficial to your liaison clients and you can use your liaison connections to introduce special collections colleagues to your faculty, researchers, and students. When I (Sha) am meeting new faculty members, I make sure to let them know about all the relevant special collections we have on our campus which are spread throughout a number of different libraries involving many different people, so it can be confusing. I offer to introduce them, making it easier for them to get connected and to help our special collections specialists make contacts with the departments I serve. Because I have worked directly and intimately with special collections, I often find opportunities when talking with students or faculty members to say things like, "Oh, if you're interested in that topic, there's a really amazing X in our special collections that I would love to share with you!" Many outreach and engagement sessions with courses and community groups have resulted from conversations that started this way. Even as I meet people in other disciplines, I have often highlighted items from special collections that might be of interest to them. More often than not, they are appreciative that you thought of them and their interests, and often it results in partnerships for teaching and collaboration. Even if I don't know of particular materials that might be of direct relevance to a faculty member, I will often offer to introduce them to one of my colleagues who can better speak to their own collections or help brainstorm ideas for collaboration. I have also partnered with special collections colleagues to create opportunities for engagement and outreach with exhibitions and public lectures (see examples in chapters 5 and 8). The main point here is that you can only have these kinds of experiences and connections if you get to know your special collections and the people who work closely with them.

Even if your special collections don't focus in areas that clearly connect with your liaison assignments, you might consider asking special collections colleagues questions like, "Does your collection have anything related to X?" Sometimes you'll be surprised at the answer, and often, your colleague will offer to explore your question, and conversations like this can be the seedbed for great partnerships and collaborations. Even if your library doesn't have huge or all-encompassing special collections, it will still be fruitful both to your constituents and to you and your colleagues to explore what these collections hold and how you might collaborate on creating outreach opportunities in courses, exhibits, or public events.[4]

To understand how liaisons have collaborated on special collections for these types of activities, see the many stories in the chapters on engagement with the humanities (chapter 5) and the arts (chapter 8).

Information Literacy and Instruction

For many, information literacy and instruction will be central to the work of liaisons. As a result, you may be tempted to skip ahead. As is often the case, when we feel like we are an expert in or have a lot of experience in an area, we tend to forget that we can benefit from others. Even old (or experienced) dogs can learn new tricks. If your institution has a formal practice of observing other instructors, that's a great way to learn from others. If your institution doesn't have a program like that, consider asking a colleague if you could sit in on their instruction session to help you improve. You might also ask a trusted colleague to sit in on your session to offer feedback. If your institution has a position dedicated to information literacy and instruction, talk with that person about ways in which they can help you grow as an instructor. Often positions like this are focused on developing literacy programs or integration into the curriculum and that can certainly lay important groundwork that you can benefit from, but such colleagues may also be willing to offer workshops for liaisons on pedagogical topics or other aspects of professional development in this area.

To read a good example of an effective collaboration between liaisons, information literacy, and special collections, see the story by Amy James.

Beyond the library, your institution may have a center or office focused on pedagogy or teaching and this can be an excellent resource for continuing professional development of liaisons. Often the programs offer workshops and seminars in which you can enroll. Not only can such offerings help you develop personally, it's also a good way to connect with faculty members on your campus and can signal to them your interest and dedication to instruction. While these centers might be primarily focused on semester-long courses and instructors of record, don't hesitate to reach out to them and discuss your particular interests, needs, and situation. At our institution, our Academy for Teaching and Learning was happy to meet with our liaisons to explore ways we could strengthen and assess our teaching. The Academy worked with us to understand the particular issues related to liaisons teaching within another person's course and in limited blocks of time.

To learn about some experiences where liaisons have collaborated across campus for information literacy and general education goals, see the story co-authored by Erin Durham, Zoe Hwang, and Elaine MacDougall, and the story by Jennifer Beach.

Partnering with Technology Specialists

While many academic libraries today include a variety of technology specialists, it's worth reiterating an earlier message: don't overlook possibilities in your own house and don't assume that just because your library might have some kinds of technology specialists, you shouldn't look out into the larger neighborhood of your institution. Wherever these specialists live organizationally, introducing your liaison clients to these specialists can increase the scope of service and support and help them in ways you can't. As with all kinds of specialists, you might ask that they keep you in the loop where possible when they've helped your liaison contacts. Just remember that this request is big and should be based on a relationship you've already built with them. It's good to remember that the technologist's primary job isn't to keep you in the loop on the clients with whom they work, especially if they live outside the library's organization and culture, and you don't want technologists to feel like you're checking up on their work. If your institution uses a customer relationship management tool, this can provide that benefit without adding tasks to the technologist's to-do list (see customer relationship management tools discussed in chapter 13).

To understand how one library has partnered their liaisons with their instructional technologists, see the story by Sarah Moazeni. To read about how one library has leveraged their expertise in technology to partner with a campus department, see the story by Chad Hutchens.

Learning Spaces Specialists

These specialists may go by many different names, but here we're identifying the technology experts who provide computer support and classroom technology support. When your constituents have questions about software, computer questions, or technology in the teaching spaces, whether in the library or in their home department, these specialists are an important resource. Be aware that academic units may have their own specialist for this whom your faculty member should work through.

As in many other relationships outlined in this chapter, your institutional culture will influence how you operate. As a liaison, do you serve as the main point of contact for your constituents no matter what library or technology needs they have? This is a model we support if it works for your setting. Rather than your new faculty member learning and navigating a long list of contacts for research help, instructional requests, interlibrary loan issues, or classroom technology issues, if you can be their source—assuming you respond quickly and help connect them to the right experts—all the better. In many cases, you as the liaison will have built relationships with your faculty, staff, and students and they may feel more comfortable asking you for help, even when you need to call in another specialist. That's perfectly fine and suggests that either you've done a good job establishing that you're someone who can help them or that they trust you, even with unfamiliar areas like technology. Some campuses, libraries, or information technology teams may be too large or complex to support this model of the liaison being the sole point of contact. The main thing to remember here is that, much like with a reference service model, or any kind of customer support for that matter, when people need help, they never want the response to be, "I can't help you with that, you'll have to contact someone else." Acceptable answers that require a technology specialist's input could be, "Let me find out for you" and you do the legwork or "That will require the expertise of another specialist. Let me put you in contact with them," either supplying all the necessary contact information or, better yet, emailing the specialist, copying the person you're helping, and introducing them with a preview of the need. Eventually, the people you serve may reach out to the specialists on their own for future needs. It doesn't always have to go through you; just know that you helped facilitate the connection well and got your client connected to the right people.

Makerspaces

Many of our readers' libraries will include some sort of makerspace. If you haven't already done so, we encourage you to visit it and talk to the people running it. Find out what technologies and tools they offer. Be thinking about any connections you can envision with your liaison constituents. Share your liaison disciplines with the makerspace staff and ask if they know of any students or faculty in those disciplines who are using the space. If not, perhaps you could brainstorm possibilities with the specialists. While some liaison disciplines may have their own departmental makerspaces, others may not, and maybe your library's makerspace has tools or expertise that the department doesn't have. This is another easy way for you to serve as a networking facilitator between other areas of the library and your constituents. Even if you don't know everything about the makerspace, you can still mention it to your students and faculty members as something that might be useful to them. It's possible they didn't know about it and it's possible that they just haven't stopped to think about how they could put it to use until you mentioned it. As you talk about it with your faculty, it may be a practical answer to a specific problem or your conversation may be broader, discussing the place of maker literacies in the larger world of literacies that the libraries support and engage with. You may even come up with ideas to incorporate into research projects, student assignments, or the curriculum.[5]

To gain insight on how just making introductions can have big payoffs, see the makerspace partnership story by Andrew Telep.

Media Spaces

New approaches to scholarship and teaching have embraced maker literacies and digital literacies and, as a result, campuses have seen tremendous growth in spaces to facilitate this. Media spaces might include checking out technical gear to clients, one-button video studios, or full production facilities for video and audio media creation. They may also include spaces and technology for augmented and virtual reality experiences.[6] In these spaces you might encounter instructors creating video modules for online classes, students creating podcasts for course assignments, or art students creating and curating art in virtual spaces. Liaisons are well positioned to partner with technology specialists, not only to stay up to date on new technologies and services, but also to help facilitate collaborations with students and faculty. Media spaces can be so much more than just the provision of tools and software; they can be the environment in which specialists and liaisons partner together to help users explore new forms of scholarship, teaching, and making.

These are but a few examples of collaborations and partnerships to consider. In addition to the following stories of collaboration, there are many other examples to explore of possibilities for liaisons to partner with other nonacademic campus units in chapter 10.

ⓖ Stories of Collaboration and Partnership

Stories can be read in the supplement at the publisher's website.
www.liaisonengagementsuccess.com

- Partnering with Peer Mentors to Engage First-Year Composition Students—by Erin Durham, Zoe Hwang, and Elaine MacDougall, University of Maryland, Baltimore County

Figure 11.2. Partnering with technology specialist Terry Raper for research and scholarship support. *Photo credit: Mary Callan Freeman*

"As the library liaison to the FYC program, Erin has found that building a partnership with the Writing Fellows has helped to scaffold sustainable information literacy support."

- Collaborating across Campus to Support Interdisciplinary Field Experiences—by Jennifer Beach, Longwood University

"Overall, initiating a liaison relationship with the Brock Experiences office at its creation proved more fruitful than many of our traditional liaison relationships, leading to a strong collaborative model that benefits the library, the courses in the Brock Experiences program, the faculty, and our students."

- Special Collections Instruction Exchange—by Amy James, Baylor University

"This group has become more than just integrating the individuals who teach from special collections and research and engagement; it has become a space for us to grow and develop as educators, as individuals, and as a team."

- Collaborations between Research and Instruction Librarians and Instructional Technologists—by Sarah Moazeni, Wellesley College

"At my institution, internal collaboration is central to our engagement model. Our team within Library and Technology Services is composed of research and instruction librarians as well as instructional technologists. Both groups have liaison responsibilities and therefore become a counterpart within our team to support teaching and learning."

- Campus Collaborations Outside of Traditional Liaison Roles—by Chad Hutchens, University of Wyoming

"I've put significant effort into how we as a department can make connections outside of the traditional liaison roles to faculty on campus because I believe we offer unique and valuable services with which most of our traditional liaisons aren't heavily engaged. Indeed, there are many ways you can build strong relationships with faculty and departments outside the bounds of the traditional subject liaison role."

- Makerspace Partnerships—by Andrew Telep, Baylor University

    "Though my group focuses principally on teaching and learning technologies, we share with liaison librarians the impulse to further discovery; assist research, teaching, and learning; promote creative uses of library resources for projects; and see faculty and students succeed. I'm grateful for the relationships our liaisons cultivate; this story started—and will continue—with people, connecting, in the library."

Key Points

- Take advantage of all the people resources at your disposal, whether they're in your department, other areas of the library, or campus and consider how the variety of potential collaborators can expand services to your liaison areas.
- Collaborate with other liaisons for interdisciplinary solutions and to fill in any skill gaps or to leverage their expertise in particular tools or approaches.
- Approach these as relationships and partnerships to develop, rather than transactional exchanges, to enable you and your collaborators institution to better support and serve your constituents.
- Consider others in your organization who, though they may not be identified as "liaisons," serve the community in specific domains and are there to support your constituents as well.
- Remember that sometimes just making introductions can open doors to unimagined partnerships and success stories.

Notes

1. For more information on the Baylor Data Scholars and the Data Research Fellows programs, see: "Digital Scholarship," Baylor University Libraries, accessed October 29, 2020, https://blogs .baylor.edu/digitalscholarship/.

2. "Data Viz of the Week," Baylor University Libraries, August 29, 2020, https://blogs.baylor .edu/digitalscholarship/data-viz-of-the-week/.

3. Association of College and Research Libraries, "Principles and Strategies for the Reform of Scholarly Communication 1," American Library Association, September 1, 2006, http://www.ala .org/acrl/publications/whitepapers/principlesstrategies.

4. Valerie A. Harris and Ann C. Weller, "Use of Special Collections as an Opportunity for Outreach in the Academic Library," *Journal of Library Administration* 52, no. 3–4 (2012): 294–303, https://doi.org/10.1080/01930826.2012.684508.

5. Katie Musick Peery, Morgan Chivers, and Tara Radniecki, "Maker Competencies and the Undergraduate Curriculum" (International Symposium on Academic Makerspaces, Stanford, CA, Higher Education Makerspace Initiative [HEMI], August 4, 2018), http://hdl.handle .net/10106/27653.

6. Christine Elliott, Marie Rose, and Jolanda-Pieta van Arnhem, eds., *Augmented and Virtual Reality in Libraries*, Library Information Technology Association (LITA) Guides (Lanham, MD: Rowman & Littlefield, 2018).

Leadership of Engaged Liaisons

LEADING LIAISONS CAN BE BOTH CHALLENGING AND REWARDING. The very thing that makes for a strong team of liaisons is often the same thing that makes leading them tricky. The best liaisons are the ones who have customized and adapted their work and skills to meet the needs of their constituents. As a group, this means that everyone's skillset and approach will be different. Of course, there are commonalities, but ultimately what a liaison for hard sciences does and thinks about may be very different from that of a liaison for performing arts. Allowing room for liaisons to develop their own individual approach to the needs of their assigned disciplines or departments can be scary and might suggest more of a loose assemblage of independent contractors. The best leaders will understand this and create space for these kinds of individualized approaches. Leading liaisons will require holding those kinds of tensions alongside the common threads shared by all liaisons and the vision for the program as a whole. Tying the work of liaisons, as disparate as that work might be, to the strategic directions of the library and the parent institution should be a crucial role of liaison leadership.

You may find yourself in a leadership role because others have recognized you as a successful liaison. If so, congratulations, but don't celebrate too long. The road ahead will be filled with challenges, but also great opportunities for growth. Begin this journey with personal reflection about your own successes as a liaison. Be sure to get input from those who have recognized your accomplishments as they may identify reasons for your success that may not be apparent to you. The results of these conversations and reflections can help develop a roadmap for you as you guide other liaisons. Be careful, however, not to view your own experience as the only route to successful engagement. A good leader will have many conversations with team members to discover areas of strength among the members that can benefit the whole. Remember, anyone who thinks they have all the answers or the only roadmap to success should be considered with suspicion. Open conversation about the hopes and fears of team members will be important for discovering areas that need more attention as well as those areas to acknowledge and celebrate. Take advantage of the experiences of others to help guide you and ask those you trust to connect you with people who can share their stories of leading liaisons, both successes and failures. We're going to recommend one to you right here to get you started. Years ago, as I (Sha) was just beginning my vocation in libraries, I worked with an exceptional student assistant, Andrea Malone, who went on to become a successful librarian. Andrea recently moved from being a liaison to leading liaisons and has written a chapter about this experience, "From Liaison to Coordinator," in the recently released book *The Academic Librarian in the Digital Age*.[1] If you're new to the world of leadership of liaisons, seek out people like Andrea and many others who can help you navigate this new journey.

Balancing Liaison Work and Leading Liaisons

One aspect that a liaison transitioning to a leadership role will surely encounter is a shift of priorities and time allotment. New administrative work will likely reduce some of the time available for actually being a liaison and this can be a hard transition. If you're asked to lead liaisons without being a liaison yourself, think very carefully about this. We fervently believe that anyone leading liaisons should still maintain some liaison role of their own, even if it's smaller than before. Discontinuing your own work as a liaison will disconnect you from those you lead and make it harder to navigate the ever-shifting waters of this work. This is especially true in a setting where the role of liaisons might be evolving. Continued involvement in liaison work gives you a chance to practice what you preach. It allows you to hone your skills, especially as skill needs evolve. Most of all, it provides a great opportunity to model for others the kind of engagement and outreach you're looking for. If you are moving into a leadership role like this, it would be wise to have open conversation with those to whom you report about expectations, opportunities, and challenges. A lack of clear understanding among all parties of the expectations and, in particular, your balance of leading and liaising, will be fraught with potential misunderstandings and hinder the good work you've been called to do.

If you find yourself charged with transitioning your organization to a more engagement-focused liaison program, you may find that you're working with liaisons at many different points on the spectrum. You may be simultaneously dealing with some people who are eager and some who are recalcitrant, and some that are just worried about what this change will mean for them. Note that the last two categories may be different manifestations of the same thing. Perhaps it's that their comfort zone is being disrupted. Maybe librarians are worried that this shift will require skills they don't have or realms of work with which they are uncomfortable. This will require patience and determination from leadership as well as the liaisons. An important aspect of this kind of change will be to focus on positive steps forward, but also a willingness to view perceived failures as an opportunity to learn and improve (see section on growth mindset). A shift in organizational focus will likely require customized growth plans or strategies to develop different areas for different librarians.

The Most Important Secret of Successful Leadership

Leaders can't be experts in everything and those who think differently or are uncomfortable with that idea will hinder the success of their own work and those they lead. Admitting that you aren't all-knowing, and learning how to leverage the skills and knowledge of others, is the best gift you can give to those you lead and to yourself. Good leaders will help build and nurture support networks that benefit liaisons. A great way to do this is through mentors. By incorporating mentors into the mix, you're not only sharing the responsibility for nurture and development, but also creating a much more fertile ground in which the liaisons can grow. Whether your institution has a formal mentoring program or not, you should always be on the lookout for ways to create and leverage these types of relationships. There's no one template for how to mentor, but here are some things we recommend considering. There is no such thing as a one-size-fits-all mentor, so don't expect to find that one person who can be an all-encompassing mentor. We're particularly fond of the idea of mentoring constellations—that is, a network of mentors, both formal and informal who can mentor in all kinds of different ways. Rather than just a 1:1 match up of mentors and new liaison, for example, consider a network of mentors that address a variety of professional and life domains. Consider how mentors can enrich the whole experience and help the mentee feel a part of the community as well as feel successful.

IT TAKES A VILLAGE

Consider multiple and different types of mentors:

- Someone from the same department who does the same kind of work
- Someone who has a lot of institutional knowledge
- Someone who is at the same stage of the journey (e.g., professionally, life situation, etc.)
- Someone from another part of the organization who can give a different perspective
- Someone who can help advise on tenure or promotion

⊚ Understanding Your Team

Like leaders in any situation, those leading liaisons will have to navigate differences, not only in the particular kinds of work, but in the individuals themselves. Smart leaders won't try to squeeze everyone into the same mold or selfishly expect everyone to adapt wholesale to the leader's own preferences for how to interact and relate to one another. This is another great opportunity to have open conversation with each liaison to work out communication approaches and working relationships. You'll have to negotiate expectations on both ends for such things as autonomy, support, and individual and group meetings. Some of the greatest potential for friction arises when assumptions are made by either person about these things or when communication isn't clear. A variety of tools for understanding types and personalities of team members can enrich individual and group understanding. Instruments like the Myers-Briggs Type Indicator, Gallup's CliftonStrengths (formerly StrengthsFinder), or the Enneagram of Personality can all shed light on how we as individuals think and act as well how we as a team can function. As a leader, these tools can help you better understand yourself as well as the dynamics between leader and team members.

RESOURCES FOR UNDERSTANDING TYPES, STRENGTHS, AND PERSONALITY

- Beatrice Chestnut, *The Nine Types of Leadership: Mastering the Art of Leadership in the 21st Century Workplace*, Franklin, TN: Post Hill Press, 2017.
- Don Riso and Russ Hudson, *Personality Types: Using the Enneagram for Self-Discovery*, Boston: Houghton Mifflin, 1996.
- The Nine Enneagram Type Descriptions, Enneagram Institute: https://www.enneagraminstitute.com/type-descriptions
- CliftonStrengths: https://www.gallup.com/cliftonstrengths/
- The sixteen MBTI types: https://www.myersbriggs.org/

⊚ Creating Customized Liaison Plans

Another useful tool for development and for articulating engagement goals is to have liaisons draft plans based on each unit with which they work, whether it's a department, school, or other organizational entity. Often a departmental plan like this will include a summary background on the unit, for example, size of faculty and students, programs and degrees, history, and areas of emphasis. Not only will this background research give the liaison a better understanding of the department, but it will help determine and contextualize the work of the liaison. A liaison plan should outline actionable steps planned for year or other division of time and align with other documents and plans of the liaison group and library. To successfully plan and achieve goals in your liaison work, you'll definitely want to create SMART goals (for more information, see sidebar). In conjunction with a framework document, these departmental plans will be an important way to track progress and identify gaps and areas requiring more attention. Leaders and liaisons should revisit these plans at regular intervals for evaluating the liaison's work and for identifying evolving needs of the liaison's constituents.

WHAT ARE SMART GOALS?

- Specific: Break goals down into smaller goals to get more specificity; vague or unclear goals are hard to track!
- Measurable: How will you tell if you're tracking or making progress?
- Achievable: Is it something that can be accomplished reasonably or realistically?
- Relevant: Does this goal help you achieve the intended purpose?
- Time bound: When will you accomplish this goal? "Someday maybe" isn't time bound and will create a loophole for never accomplishing the goal.

RESOURCES FOR SMART GOALS

- University of California: Smart Goals: A How to Guide https://tinyurl.com/UCsmartgoals
- SMART Goals: How to Make Your Goals Achievable https://www.mindtools.com/pages/article/smart-goals.htm
- Setting SMART Goals for Smart Staff Development https://digital.library.unt.edu/ark:/67531/metadc102298/

Frameworks for Liaison Work

If your team has an existing framework for liaison work, congratulations! Such a framework serves as a roadmap to keep everyone moving in the same direction, even if the details vary among individual liaison assignments. The framework should articulate major areas of emphasis important to your setting, such as research services, subject knowledge, scholarly communications, teaching and learning, collections, and outreach and engagement. For each of the focus areas, the framework should include an explanation of core activities and examples of best practices for these core activities. A framework can help teams work in agreed upon directions while minimizing gaps in service. Liaisons can use this important tool to plan individual goals and activities. It's great to say, "I plan to work more on scholarly communication this year," but even better if you can look to a framework that codifies important aspects and offers concrete examples of actions that you could incorporate. For an example of a liaison framework with core activities and best practices, see the "Liaison Framework for the Research and Engagement Librarians of Baylor University."[2] In addition, the section on "Creating a Shared Vision for Engagement" later in this chapter describes the process we took to create this framework.

The following sections highlight several important areas of focus for liaisons. They are drawn from the framework created at Baylor University[3] and are highly informed by many other frameworks that came before it. It's important to note here that frameworks, like other things mentioned previously, aren't "one size fits all." There are likely many areas that will be common to most frameworks across all institutions, but your framework should focus on areas that are most important to the work in your particular context. As you can see from the following table, some institutions include areas that may or may not be relevant to your situation. Liaisons may be involved in additional areas that fall outside the role of liaison work. You'll want to decide whether those aspects belong in your liaison framework or other documentation. If you don't already have a framework for liaisons, we strongly encourage you to create one collaboratively with involvement from your liaisons and library leadership. The most useful framework will be a living document that you, library leadership, and the liaisons themselves revisit regularly, reviewing, updating, and evolving to best reflect the work that your liaisons are called to do in the context of your setting.

Outreach and Engagement

You might be thinking, "Isn't this whole book about outreach and engagement? Why is there a specific section on this?" The answer is threefold: first, it's important. Second, because all of the other sections that follow could be addressed without a specific mindset of outreach and engagement, we feel as though it needs its own section in this discussion or in a framework. Third, while many of the activities and approaches in outreach and engagement pair with or become the vehicle through which we can make strides in the other areas, they can be independent of those actions.

The overarching goal within outreach and engagement is to "consistently and strategically engage our constituents to promote mutual understanding of the libraries' role in achieving the mission of the university."[4] Everything else we recommend for your consideration in the work of liaisons should be viewed through that lens. Whether you're dealing with collections, services, or programs, the liaison is the ambassador of the much larger and strategically driven operation. Successful outreach and engagement for a liaison may include things like:

- Building good networks between their faculty and students and experts in library and technology domains
- Working with collections, cataloging, and metadata teams to improve access to resources
- Maintaining a visible presence in departments through mobile reference, research consultations, regular visits, and attending departmental events
- Working with marketing and communication teams (whether in the department, library, or institution) to effectively promote services and resources
- Engaging with relevant student organizations as a show of support or as an advisor, or mentor

Subject Knowledge

Rare is the institution in which liaisons have advanced degrees in each discipline they serve. Often, liaisons will have varied and diverse portfolios that include subject areas outside of their own academic training. Leaders should encourage liaisons to build an understanding of the disciplines they serve in a variety of ways that make sense for the situation. Unless it's built into your institutional culture and job expectations, it may not be reasonable to expect liaisons to pursue advanced degrees or certifications in the disciplines they serve. While this might be valuable, there are certainly other ways to build dis-

Table 12.1. Categories of work in liaison frameworks

UNIVERSITY OF MARYLAND LIBRARIES	UNIVERSITY OF MINNESOTA LIBRARIES	UNIVERSITY OF IOWA LIBRARIES	THE OHIO STATE UNIVERSITY LIBRARIES	DUKE UNIVERSITY LIBRARIES	DARTMOUTH LIBRARY	BAYLOR UNIVERSITY LIBRARIES
Guidelines for subject librarian liaisons	Librarian Position Description Framework	Iowa Framework for Liaisons/ Subject Librarians	A framework for the engaged librarian: Building on our strengths	Engaging with Library Users: Sharpening our Vision as Subject Librarians for the Duke University Libraries	Dartmouth college library liaisons: Engaging with our community	Liaison Framework for the Research and Engagement Librarians of Baylor University
2008	2009	2009	2011	2011	2013	2017
Communication	Campus Engagement	Overall Liaison Activities	Engagement	Engagement	Engagement	Outreach and Engagement
Reference/ Consultation	"Ask Us" Services	Reference & Research Services	Research Services	Research Services	Research Services	Research Services
Collection Development	Content/Collections	Collection Development and Management	Collection Development	Collection Development	Collection Development	Collections
Subject Library Instruction	Teaching and Learning	Teaching and Learning	Teaching and Learning	Teaching and Learning	Education and Outreach	Teaching and Learning
Mastery of the Subject						Subject Knowledge
	Scholarly Communication	Scholarly Communication	Scholarly Communication	Scholarly Communication	Scholarly Communication	Scholarly Communications
	E-Scholarship and Digital Tools			Digital Tools	Digital Tools	
	Outreach	Outreach (external)		Outreach to Constituencies beyond Duke University*	Education and Outreach	
	Fund Raising	Fund Raising*		Fundraising/Grants Management*		
	Exhibit and Event Planning*			Exhibits*	Exhibits	
	Leadership					
	Management and Supervision*	Management and Supervision*		Technical Services*	Technical and Access Support Services	
						* depends upon specific job descriptions

ciplinary knowledge, such as webinars, conferences, departmental lectures, and directed readings. Leaders should work with liaisons to build a roadmap for continuing education and professional development related to liaison assignments. It's important to note that all of these paths to deepening subject knowledge provide opportunities for engagement with faculty and students with whom the liaison works. I (Sha) am the liaison to the art department at my institution and I'm also the founder and curator of the book arts collection in our library. This special collection has afforded me many opportunities to build connections with faculty members and their students. Because of this collection, a faculty member with whom I've built a great relationship invited me to be embedded in a book arts seminar she was teaching. During the course, students studied examples from the collection, learned many relevant skills for creating their own artist's books, and launched a successful exhibition at the end of the semester. Because of my engaged participation in the course, I developed my own skills alongside the students and moved beyond my role as a collection curator to finding my own voice as a practicing artist in this medium. This experience sparked my own creative work, resulting in the creation of several artist's books that have been selected for several international juried art exhibitions and books that have been collected by institutions and private collectors through the country. While this in-depth experience with the course helped me to deepen my own knowledge in the discipline I serve as a librarian, it also provided rich engagement opportunities with faculty and students in that discipline and positive relationships that continue years later. While certainly every liaison's experience will not result in them becoming a practitioner in the discipline field, you can help liaisons explore paths for enriching their work and their engagement with their constituents by investigating ways to deepen knowledge of the subject matter, whether it's at the broad discipline level or micro level, such as a particular aspect directly related to how the liaison is engaging with the faculty or students. This type of development often has huge pay offs in networking and relationship building with the faculty and students as they see and appreciate the librarian's efforts to better understand their world and work.

Other important ways to strengthen a liaison's understanding of the discipline are more closely tied to the departments they are serving. One way to do this is for liaisons to familiarize themselves with the research areas among the faculty. Get to know the existing publications of your faculty and, as you build relationships with them, you'll likely have an awareness of their current research areas and needs. By analyzing trends in departmental teaching, curricula, and new courses offered, you'll not only build your understanding of important topics and domains in the field, but also have a better understanding of the direction of the programs, and often, in the case of upper-level seminars, a good window into specific areas of interest of the faculty members. Other easy wins for continuing to expand your subject knowledge includes monitoring relevant discipline-related listservs, joining relevant academic and professional associations, auditing courses, and attending departmental lectures and symposia.

Research Services

Research services is an area everyone expects to be a part of the work of liaisons—so much so that you might be tempted to think "of course, I get it, research support is what we do and have always done" and decide to skip this section. We would urge you to shed any assumptions you have about this domain and consider thoughtfully the expanding and evolving nature of this work and, if you're leading liaisons, to help them do the same.

Some practices may be new to your experience, and while some may be familiar, we challenge you to reevaluate the latter to see if there are improvements or adaptations to consider. One part of successful research services is, of course, to provide specialized research support. Recommendations already made in the subject knowledge section should inform thoughtful work in this most fundamental level of research services. It's easy to rely on sources you discovered or mastered early on in your work (whether in library school or on-the-job training, but make sure you, and any liaisons you influence, don't stop there. It's also easy to let modern technologies carry the load, like aggregated databases, or A-Z lists of databases, or even just focusing a surface-level operational understanding of databases. Don't let knowing how to filter or export records, or craft Boolean strings, or find full-text articles stand in for your understanding the language or terminology of the discipline and its overarching concepts.

Another aspect of this domain that might feel a little obvious is research consultations. That won't be a new idea to anyone, but we challenge you to think about the way you offer this service. Is it a reactive measure to someone approaching a reference desk? Is it a secret service offered to those brave enough to call or email you and ask? How proactive and advertised is this service? How pervasive and easy is it for your constituents? While there are tools and technologies to help with all these questions, they aren't required to make your service better but they do certainly make it much easier. While not the only tools to do this, Springshare's suite of online tools offers a great example of how you can make your services more dynamic and proactive. Tools like this make it really easy to communicate with your researchers, advertise availability of liaisons for research appointments, and streamline scheduling and follow-up. Offering research consultations in the department is a great way to advertise proactive services, although it does depend on the culture and facilities of the department. Departments may be able to offer you hoteling space or a dedicated consultation space. Other options include pop-up consultation offerings in public spaces frequented by students or faculty. As a leader, you might help liaisons assess the situation, offer to help request space, and in some cases provide support for liaisons offering consultations onsite in a department. Examples of this might include technology like a tablet, laptop, or second monitor, or things like a table and signage. Maybe it involves negotiating storage space in the department. Other ways to support liaisons in this work is to encourage and acknowledge successes and experiments and champion this work with library administration and to the academic departments. Whatever the details, think about how you can encourage and support liaisons in this way, even if it's just to test the waters. Sometimes these kinds of experiments work great and sometimes they fail. Be open to learning about why something didn't work and don't be afraid to adapt or abort as needed.

Scholarly Communication

Scholarly communication is in many ways an extension of research services or even part and parcel, but we've separated it here for a couple reasons. First, some institutions will have separate scholarly communication units and some will have teams that overlap liaisons and professionals from other areas. Regardless of how it's handled at your institution, it's important to be familiar with scholarly communication and ways in which liaisons can be involved. One way that scholarly communication is viewed differently from traditional research services is that the latter might be seen, intentionally or not, as focused on the traditional and earliest stages of research, including things like finding sources and compiling literature reviews, whereas scholarly communication includes other, later parts of the research process, such as copyright, licensing, and open-access publishing. This focus on the entire life cycle of research may be new to some liaisons and those whose training and experience centers in a more traditional reference service model. Authors Sarah Anne Murphy and Craig Gibson note the importance of "expanding the traditional liaison model into the workflows of faculty and students to touch 'upstream' and 'downstream' phases of the research process." They go on to articulate this important point: "Liaison librarians who actively participate in more stages of the research process and the creation of knowledge through the provision of an integrated suite of research services will become more engaged with users." Research services may best be envisioned as an emerging model of research life cycle–focused support—expanding the traditional repertoire of reference skills and research consultations into a more fully engaged participation, at a programmatic level, across the spectrum of research activities on campus.[5]

For some, championing scholarly communication issues may be focused on advertising and promoting the work of a dedicated scholarly communication librarian or unit. For others, it may require acquiring new skills and new competencies. Sometimes this work will require new approaches at early stages of research, such as helping researchers identify and access data sets or helping guide them in data management issues. At the other end of the research life cycle, liaisons can help navigate alternative publication models such as digital repositories and open-access journals. This can get complicated, however. Departmental or institutional cultures may be skeptical of, or worse hostile to, these "new" modes of publication as they don't always align with traditional practices of tenure and promotion. Often, institutions rely on established and widely accepted publication venues to count for tenure and promotion. It's important for liaisons to have, where possible, an understanding of existing departmental guidelines and expectations. Encouraging an unsuspecting new faculty member to focus on open-access journals, could, in fact, harm their tenure and promotion process. We encourage liaisons to help push the envelope as they are able, but also to be sensitive to the complex issues at play. We also encourage liaisons to dialog with leaders in the academic unit (chairs, deans, associate deans, as well as respected and established tenured faculty members who are open to evolving modes of and platforms for scholarship). These conversations can help educate, create awareness of issues, and build understanding for all parties involved. Where liaisons uncover roadblocks to open access issues, remember that there are many aspects of scholarly communication to support such as data management, copyright, and licensing. One important way you can lead liaisons in areas of scholarly communication is by supporting educational opportunities, facilitating networks with experts in relevant areas, and encouraging liaisons to build competencies and skills in these areas.

Teaching and Learning

While teaching has long been a part of liaison responsibilities (even back when we were called reference librarians!), there are some distinctive characteristics of this type of work for engaged liaisons. No longer are librarians regurgitating canned, tried-and-true spiels about how to use the library catalog to find resources for traditional research papers, when a professor requests a session by the librarian. The kind of instruction more common to engaged liaisons is marked by collaboration with instructors-of-record to design and deliver a variety of new types of instruction in a variety of modes. Much less a "tour of databases," successful instruction is now more frequently reflecting pedagogical grounding and curricular integration. Maybe your institution is fortunate enough to have an established curriculum-mapping enterprise or a librarian dedicated to information literacy initiatives. Perhaps your campus has a center or office focused on the advancement of teaching and learning. If you have any of those, definitely take advantage of them. Even if you feel as though an institutional office was designed more for semester-long courses or instructors of record, reach out to them and discuss opportunities for partnership or learning. At our campus, the Academy for Teaching and Learning was more than happy to partner with our liaison program to investigate the kind of teaching we were doing and what we hoped to gain from conversations with their team, and then they provided a helpful assessment of where we were along with ideas for us to consider implementing to continue growing and developing our teaching. If you don't have access to programs or personnel like those listed here, there are still plenty of ways liaisons can develop their teaching. No matter how small your teaching moment, even if it's only one class session or a part of a session, think about what you're teaching and what the learning objectives are as well as how you're organizing and delivering the information. Whenever possible, discuss all this with the instructor of record to ensure you are in agreement on the objectives and approaches. If you're leading liaisons, even from within the pack, you might suggest holding a bring-your-lunch discussion to talk through ideas and strategies to move in this direction. Don't forget about supplementing other venues for development with a world of helpful publications, listservs, discussion groups, and webinars that can help develop in these areas.

Collections

Collection building has long been a familiar domain for many liaisons, although for many, the landscape has been shifting. While some institutions have historically had, and some still have, full-time bibliographers, many institutions have relied on reference librarians or liaisons to fill this role. Daniel C. Mack paints a vivid picture of this role when he writes, "At most institutions the day is long since past when bibliographers sat in offices in the back of the stacks, surrounded by publisher's catalogs and occasionally consulting with faculty."[6] While institutions will have personnel to manage many of the details of the work of ingesting, cataloging, and processing collections materials, often liaisons are charged with some level of collections-related work. It's important to have a clear understanding of your institutional direction in this arena so that liaisons aren't working at cross purposes with a larger strategic plan. In some cases, liaisons are monitoring or managing requests from their faculty or in their assigned subject areas. For others, collection work has moved from a granular, title-level focus to a more macro focus like recommending datasets, databases, or large packages. Of course, the strategic direction and philosophy of collecting is heavily influenced, if not driven, by space and money, and this is often part of the shifting sands of collection work for liaisons. Regardless of the landscape at your institution, liaisons can approach collections in their work in a number of ways. Communicating with the departments to understand their ongoing needs is really important, but so is the liaison's understanding of the library's philosophy on collections. Maybe your institution continues to build what we like to call "old school" collections, from a mythical time when libraries sought to build the largest, most comprehensive collections possible. Maybe your institution has a different approach—because of space, money, accessibility, the internet, or user needs—that dictates not trying to collect everything, but instead focusing only on getting people access to what they need when they need it. These very different approaches, and all the in-between possibilities, dramatically change the way liaisons might work in collections. Often liaisons will find that their library's direction is at odds with the expectations of the faculty with whom they work. In those situations, it's important that the liaison understands the landscape and how best to communicate with their constituents. Regardless of your institution's collection strategies or the size of your budget or collections, liaisons can and should use their collections as a basis for engagement with their faculty and students. Acquiring any resources, regardless of format, is a waste of time and money if liaisons are not actively exploring ways to connect users to these resources. Maybe you know someone who has added material to the collection and then quickly moved on to the next thing the collection needed. Maybe they've thought, "This database seems really useful and I'm sure my faculty and students would appreciate my adding to our collection," and then they moved on to tackling the endless list of other important things a liaison does. Here's the rub though: if you place orders like that and never look back, you've wasted your time and your institution's resources. Think about how you can make the most of the investment by making sure to publicize the new resource and even contextualize it. Think "why should I care about or use this?" We're not saying to have an ad campaign for every book you add, but be mindful of the fact that hidden and unused resources are, for all intents and purposes, worthless. Another way of saying this is "know what you have and think about how to share that knowledge." You'll be a better liaison and your students and faculty will be richer for it. Engaging with your communities will help you make better informed decisions about resources to acquire or highlight. There are many more ideas of how liaisons can navigate the turbulent waters of collection development work to be found in the framework documents that have been mentioned here, and we encourage you as a liaison leader to explore them and have conversations with colleagues and library leadership about the institution's goals and your role helping achieve those. If you're leading liaisons, your job will be to clearly understand the institution's goals, the tension points that will inevitably surface with academic departments, the variability among disciplines and how they interact with resources, and helping your liaisons find a productive path forward in this area.

◎ Creating a Shared Vision for Engagement

Because successful liaison work will be customized to the needs and cultures of specific constituencies, it's easy for liaisons to function like a loose federation of independent contractors. However, it will be important for everyone to be working in the same direction with the goals of the institution and the library in clear sight. The job of those leading liaisons will be to hold this tension in balance and to fashion a road map that can accommodate both aspects.

In 2013, we began investigating ways to better understand ourselves as individuals and how that influences our own work and the dynamics of the teams to which we belong. This work was not limited to liaisons, but included various public service teams of our Research and Engagement department. We invited everyone in the department to take the StrengthsFinder assessment (now CliftonStrengths by Gallup) through our university's human resources department. This instrument seeks to uncover the most prominent strengths of the individual with 34 themes across four domains of executing, influencing, relationship building, and strategic thinking. We then held an afternoon retreat for the department, led by our Human Resources consultant, to gain a better understanding of the strengths and domains reflected in the instrument and the distribution of strengths throughout the department. The results of this experience helped all of our team better understand themselves and how they related to the entire team. It helped explain some tension points in our working relationships and roadblocks to success. For our liaisons and for our leadership team, it helped us see why some parts of liaison work came easily while other parts were more difficult or challenging.

In creating a shared vision specifically around the work of liaisons, it's important to have buy-in from all of the involved parties if you want the plan to be successful. This will require lots of time and conversation, but in the end, will result in a stronger plan. For us, this journey began with a lunch conversation between the two of us at a library conference. We discussed how we might envision some structure and guidance for our team of liaisons while still affirming the individuality found in each of our work. We gathered a list of relevant readings as well as a list of libraries that had already begun clearing a path in the direction we wanted to go. We knew we needed to talk through the various pieces of this project, give people time to read the documents, and gather input and ideas from all the liaisons, if we wanted this effort to succeed. To create space and time for this project, we developed a day-long retreat, off campus, where the liaisons could gather free of distractions and interruptions to focus on this work.

One of the activities we planned for this retreat was designed to help liaisons think about their existing networks and interactions with their faculty members. We provided lists of each department with all of the current faculty members and asked each liaison to jot down interactions they had with as many of the faculty as possible, even interactions that fell outside of liaison work. We then spread the lists throughout the large room where we were meeting and asked all of us to peruse all the lists, even those that weren't our own departments, and add any connections we might have with other faculty members. The responses included things like, "I went through faculty orientation with this person," "We served on a committee together," "We're neighbors!," "We met at the local dog park," "Our kids attend the same school," and "We're in a dinner club together." This exercise not only helped each of us to consider the many kinds of connections we have to people in our campus community, but also helped us see connections that our colleagues have. Understanding these connections have yielded conversations between liaisons that have strengthened relationships with our constituents. For example, "Oh, since you know this professor really well, can you introduce me?" or "Since you've worked with one of my faculty members in another context, maybe we could partner together on this project."

Prior to the retreat, we'd shared guiding documents related to the work of liaisons from the following institutions: University of Maryland, University of Minnesota, University of Iowa, Penn State, Ohio State, and Dartmouth. During the retreat, we identified a number of overarching categories of liaison work and placed these on large sheets of paper spread around the room. As a group, we added to the category lists from our own experiences and the guiding documents. We spent time individually reviewing and reflecting on the work and then voting, by "dotmocracy," for activities that best represented each category. After lunch, one of our colleagues led a session on SMART goals (see sidebar and resources on SMART goals earlier in this chapter). We finished the afternoon by spreading out throughout the retreat facility to spend individual time working on liaison plans for each of our assigned departments. For more on this, see the previous section in this chapter on "Creating Customized Liaison Plans."

Over the next several months, we divided our liaisons into working groups, each with an assigned category from the retreat. We tasked these groups with aggregating descriptions, bullet points, and best practices from the retreat brainstorming and the guiding documents. The working groups then drafted an overarching description of their assigned area and recommended best practices. All liaisons had opportunities to review and comment on the documents created by each working group, after which a final editorial team reviewed the entire framework document. The process began in early summer with the initial conversation and lasted throughout the remainder of the fall semester, at which point we delivered the finalized framework document to the library administration.

Key Points

- Find the balance between leading the work of the liaison group and being a great liaison yourself.
- Approach your leadership with humility and a mindset of growth.
- Identify mentors for your own development.
- Consider the variety of tools and resources to better understand your team members so that you can appreciate their gifts, their needs, and how you can help them succeed.
- Celebrate and leverage individual strengths and skills of each liaison while also finding the common ground shared among all liaisons.
- Develop a framework for liaisons to guide the work of the team and the individual.

Notes

1. Andrea Malone, "From Liaison to Coordinator: How Digital Humanities Influenced a Role Change and Restructure," in *Academic Librarian in the Digital Age: Essays on Changing Roles and Responsibilities*, ed. Tom Diamond (Jefferson, NC: McFarland, 2020).

2. Sha Towers et al., "Liaison Framework for the Research and Engagement Librarians of Baylor University," Working Paper, accessed November 5, 2020, https://hdl.handle.net/2104/11086.

3. Towers et al., "Liaison Framework."

4. Towers et al., "Liaison Framework," 7.

5. Sarah Anne Murphy and Craig Gibson, "Informing the Evolution of an Engaged Liaison Librarian Model," in *Assessing Liaison Librarians Documenting Impact for Positive Change*, ed. Daniel C. Mack and Gary W. White, Publications in Librarianship 67 (Chicago: Association of College and Research Libraries, 2014), 17–18.

6. Daniel C. Mack, "Beyond the Bibliographer: Assessing Collection Development Activities in the New Digital Library," in *Assessing Liaison Librarians Documenting Impact for Positive Change*, ed. Daniel C. Mack and Gary W. White, Publications in Librarianship 67 (Chicago: Association of College and Research Libraries, 2014), 71.

CHAPTER 13

Assessment and Evaluation of Engaged Librarians

AS A LEADER OF ENGAGED LIAISONS, you've considered the goals of your institution and your library and you've developed the perfect framework to guide the work of your liaisons. You have a plan, but that's just the beginning. Your next steps will be to figure out how you'll know if what you set out to do is actually what's happening and if your plans are successful. Mack and White write,

> The twenty-first-century academic library requires an ongoing, pro-active, and relevant program of assessment for its liaison librarians. The outcomes of such a program will ensure that the library's suite of services remains central to the teaching mission and research enterprise of the university. Properly conducted and incorporated into a professional development program, assessment can transform good librarians into great librarians.[1]

Assessment versus Evaluation

So how do we assess and evaluate the work of liaisons? First let's look at these two terms. While they are related, and often used interchangeably, it's helpful to view them as distinct from one another. *Assessment* is the observation or determination of the current state or what is happening at that moment, as in the phrase "assess the situation." We're gathering information to understand what we're observing. *Evaluation* is what we do with that which we've assessed, determining significance or assigning value. If you think about a test you might take in a history class, the test itself is an assessment of what you have learned or what you know. It is a data gathering instrument. When an instructor grades the test, they are evaluating the results of the assessment to determine if you achieved a predefined goal of knowledge mastery and to assign value or a grade. Therefore, before we can evaluate the work of liaisons, we need an instrument, or an assessment tool. Looking again at our test analogy, the assessment tool, the test, has been designed to measure performance against an established set of goals, namely information on a topic or synthesis of understanding on a given topic that is expected from the student, or to establish a baseline of knowledge on a subject. This instrument is designed to help determine the scope or breadth of knowledge or understanding on a topic. In the same way, an assessment of liaison work should help us determine the nature and scope of that work. Our history test was not created in a vacuum, however. Hopefully it has been based on material relevant to the course, and the course exists because it was determined to be relevant to a curriculum, which is often based on broader goals and decisions of some governing body that has established domains of what students should learn. If we create tests first and then worked backward toward a curriculum, we've got the cart before the horse. In the same way, we should think carefully about the overarching objectives for a liaison program before we can successfully evaluate the work of individual liaisons.

Articulating Goals

Whether you inherited an established liaison program or have been charged with developing one, you should begin by identifying and articulating the goals of the program. While it might seem easy to adopt goals from another institution, it's crucial to consider the context of your institution and library. The development of program aims should begin in consultation with library leadership and, where possible, the liaisons themselves. Resnis and Natale note, "Outcomes for the program should be clear, able to be assessed, and should reflect what the group of liaisons wants to accomplish together."[2] Any successful assessment plan should include these three components:

- Outcomes—"the ultimate results desired or actually achieved"
- Processes—"the programs, services and activities developed to produce the desired outcomes"
- Inputs—"resources, including faculty, staff, and students, finances, and facilities and other physical resources"[3]

While we've talked earlier about the high variability in the work of liaisons based on the needs and cultures of the departments they serve, it's important to have programmatic goals that are universal for all liaisons. Program-level goals should reflect any existing framework for liaisons or inform the creation of such a framework. These goals should align with those of the library and institution. Start by thinking about what you and the library leadership want the liaison program to achieve and make sure it's explicitly tied to the library's and institution's goals and objectives.

⊚ Using the Right Tools

If your role includes evaluating the work of liaisons, you've likely thought about how the fact that different departments need different things and how liaisons have different skill sets complicates your job quite quickly. This department only wants data from the last two years while that department concentrates on sources from before the printing press. This liaison has mastered data management skills, while that liaison has mastered pedagogical approaches for information literacy. This liaison creates many online modules, but that liaison teaches all in-person instruction sessions. To begin, don't get sidetracked by the diversity of personalities, products, and accomplishments. Imagine if you were judging a tomato contest at a county fair. Tomatoes come in all different shapes, sizes, and colors. While they're all from the same plant (*Solanum lycopersicum*), and all point toward the same end of getting ripe and being eaten, they go about those life goals in different ways. You wouldn't fault a yellow variety for not turning bright red. You wouldn't say to a cherry tomato, "Why aren't you large enough to fit on a sandwich?" In the same way, look at the big picture goals (Is this a ripe and delicious tomato?), but also acknowledge the unique features and how well they are suited to the task at hand.

Assessing Tools Currently in Use

Some of the kinds of assessment you should consider might seem obvious, but that doesn't make them any less important. How many instructional sessions are liaisons teaching? How many research consultations? How are you capturing this data? What instruments are you using to assess what's happening? Is everyone maintaining their own "tick marks"? Are liaisons relying on their calendars and inboxes to know what their activity looks like? You first task might just be assessing what instruments are currently in use and if those tools are effectively accomplishing what they need to. At our institution, we created templates using Springshare's LibInsights tool. One template tracks instruction (figure 13.1) and the other tracks liaison activity reflective of our liaison framework (figure 13.2). For each, individual liaisons record their own activity, but the beauty of a template interface to a dataset like these is that they also provide aggregated, program-level views of the data.

Figure 13.1.

Date of Session *	[ ] 🗓
Length (duration) of Session *	Select a value ▾
Session Type *	Select a value ▾
Session Location	Select a value ▾
Library Specific Location (if applicable)	Select a value ▾
other Location	[ ]
Course Prefix	[ ]
Course Number and Section	[ ]
Course Name *	[ ]
Instructor of Record # 1	[ ]
Instructor of Record # 2	[ ]
Number of Participants *	[ ]
Library Instructor	Select a value ▾
Other Library Instructors (select all)	Filgo, Ellen / Fisher, Amanda / Fisher, Paul / French, Laura / Goolsby, Mary

Type of Instruction	☐ Active Learning/Assignments -- students worked in groups or individually to explore or complete assigned activities and tasks
	☐ Directed Practice -- students followed along on their computers and performed tasks, e.g. using certain search terms and strategies suggested by librarian
	☐ Demonstration
	☐ Flipped Instruction - Flipped Instruction provides instruction material and content for students to complete prior to the class or outside of the classroom (often online). It allows more in-class time to be spent on learning activities.
	☐ Lecture
	☐ Tour/Orientation
Is this a new session? *	○ Yes ○ No
Is this an existing session that was substantially revised? *	○ Yes ○ No ○ N/A
Did you create a new research guide? *	○ Yes ○ No
If you used a Research Guide, new or existing, enter URL here	[ ]
Did you conduct an assessment? *	○ Yes ○ No
If you included any type of assessment, please explain or provide link to assessment form here:	[ ]
General Comments	[ ]

Figure 13.1.   Instruction data, Baylor University Libraries

Start Date	[ ]
Date of Activity *	[ ] 🗓
Brief Description	[ ]
More Details	[ ]
Non-Liaison Activity	☐ Library Meeting
	☐ Library Event/Exhibit
	☐ Library Committee Work
	☐ Collection Development
	☐ Collection Management
	☐ Administrative / Personnel
	☐ Online Content
	☐ Professional Development
	☐ Creating Scholarship
	☐ Library Training
	☐ Service to the University
	☐ Service to the Community
	☐ Service to the Profession
Non-Liaison Location:	Select a value ▾
Time spent on this non-liaison activity:	Select a value ▾

Liaison Activity	☐ Liaison Networking
	☐ Dept. Event
	☐ Collections
	☐ Promotion of Library
	☐ Course Support
	☐ Course Guide/Content
	☐ Citation Management
	☐ Research Support
	☐ Scholarly Communication Support
	☐ Tech Support
	☐ Digital Scholarship Support
	☐ Funding Support
	☐ Tenure Process Support
	☐ Library Stats/Reports
	☐ Mobile Ref
Initiator of contact	○ client ○ librarian
Client type	Select a value ▾
Department	Select a value ▾
Univ. Services Dept.	Select a value ▾
Contact Method	Select a value ▾
Contact Method - OTHER	[ ]
Is this a referral?	Select a value ▾
Liaison Location	Select a value ▾
Time spent on this liaison activity:	Select a value ▾

Figure 13.2.   Liaison activity template, Baylor University Libraries

Tracking Liaison Connections with Clients

Another approach that may be helpful for gathering data about the work of your liaisons is the use of a customer relationship management (CRM) tool. While certainly not the only example, Springshare's LibCRM is a good example of a CRM platform designed specifically for libraries. Incorporating a CRM into your ecosystem can illuminate client needs and how your team is addressing those needs with the added benefit of tracing relationship and service networks. For example, such a tool might shed light on how the libraries are connecting and serving a particular faculty member even beyond the work of their own liaison. Maybe they've also worked with a digital scholarship specialist, an archivist, and a copyright specialist in addition to their liaison. An awareness of all of these contact points can strengthen the work of the liaison, not to mention the entire service model of the library. Incorporating a CRM tool can add to the kinds of data you collect to analyze and evaluate the work of your team.

CRM TOOLS

- LibCRM (Springshare) https://www.springshare.com/libcrm/
  - Created for and mainly used by academic libraries.
- Savannah (OrangeBoy) https://www.orangeboyinc.com/savannah
  - Created for and mainly used by public libraries.
- Patron Point (Patron Point, Inc.) https://www.patronpoint.com/
  - Created for and mainly used by public libraries.
- Salesforce (Salesforce.com, Inc.) https://www.salesforce.com/
  - Created for and mainly used in business settings.
- Zoho CRM (Zoho Corporation) https://www.zoho.com/crm/
  - Created for and mainly used in business settings.

Tracking Research Consultation Activity

Following each research consultation with our liaisons, the consultee automatically receives a follow-up survey (figure 13.3). Our team created this form with Springshare's LibApps suite (created in LibWizard as follow-up to appointments scheduled through LibCal) and designed it to capture the type of consultation, the classification and affiliation of the scheduler, and how the scheduler perceived the relevance and success of the consultation.

In addition to these quantitative questions, consider what qualitative ones you should be asking. Do you have a way to gather feedback from faculty or students on instruction or on research consultations? If so, what kinds of questions are you asking? Are the questions going to get at what you're trying to assess? When you look at the responses, individually or collectively, do they give you information that's useful? Here is an example of the feedback form that we use following instruction sessions, created in Qualtrics (figure 13.4).

LibCal Appointment Follow-Up

BAYLOR | University Libraries

HOME | RESEARCH | GET HELP | LIBRARIES | SERVICES | ABOUT | GIVE | Search our site...

Name (optional):

I am a: (required)
Make a selection ▼

What is your major or department? (required)
Make a selection ▼

How did you hear about making an appointment with a librarian? (required)
☐ Librarian, personally
☐ Librarian, during a class
☐ Professor
☐ Friend
☐ Library website
☐ Information/Service desk in the library
☐ Other

Why did you make an appointment? (required)
☐ Confused about my assignment
☐ Needed help with the research process
☐ Needed help finding sources
☐ Needed help finding a specific source
☐ Needed help with citation
☐ Seeking digital scholarship assistance
☐ Other

Did you learn something new about the library's resources during your appointment with a librarian? (required)
○ Yes
○ No

If you learned something new, what was it?

How well did the appointment meet your information needs? (required)
○ Not well at all
○ Mildly well
○ Fairly well
○ Very well
○ Extremely well

Would you recommend making an appointment with a librarian to others? (required)
○ Yes
○ No

If so, why?

Submit

Figure 13.3. Research consultation appointment follow-up survey, Baylor University Libraries

What class or workshop was your library session for? (ex. Zotero Workshop, ENG 2301, THEA 3326)

If this session is course affiliated, who is your professor? (last name, first name)

Which library instructor(s) taught your session? (hold Ctrl to select multiple instructors)

Eric Ames
Joshua Been
Eileen Bentsen
Stephen Bolech
Jennifer Borderud
Susan Bowlin
David Burns
Adrienne Cain
Ken Carriveau
Christina Chan-Park

In your opinion, did today's session meet its objectives?
○ Yes
○ No
○ I'm not sure what the objectives were.

How useful was the information presented in the session?
○ Very useful
○ Pretty useful (I'll probably use most of this in the future)
○ Somewhat useful
○ Slightly useful
○ Not useful

Did today's session improve your skills or provide you with tools that will help you for your class, assignments, projects, etc.?
○ Yes
○ No

What did you like most about the session?

What could have been improved in today's session?

Please provide your email if you would like any followup (not required).

→

Powered by Qualtrics ℠

Figure 13.4. Postinstruction survey, Baylor University Libraries

Establishing a Baseline

Whether you're creating a program for assessment or whether such a program already exists, but you're new to coordinating it, it's important to establish some kind of baseline. Don't fret about the fact that you think your liaison program should be offering more instructional sessions or more research consultations. First have a clear understanding of where you are; that is, assess the situation. Maybe you're not supporting all the departments on campus just yet or maybe you'd like to see more proactive outreach from the liaisons. Without a baseline of the current situation, you don't know where your program is on the journey toward its goals.

If you start with institutional-level goals and build assessment tools that match these, you should be well positioned to gather data not only at the programmatic level, but at the individual liaison level as well. As illustrated in figure 13.2, our liaison activity dataset allows us to see the types of activities for each liaison, the level to which they serve each of their assigned departments, and the activities particular to each department or level of users such as undergraduate, graduate, and faculty. The dataset also indicates where the engagement is taking place and who is initiating the contact. Not only will you want a baseline for the program, but you'll want a baseline for individual liaisons and the departments they serve. This might be based on a liaison's previous record, or in the case of a new liaison, the baseline might be to assess how the assigned department was served previously.

Telling the Story

As you begin to evaluate the data you've collected, think about the narrative you will create. This contextualization is crucial. If you know that your liaisons taught 2,000 instructional sessions this year, that might sound impressive, but it depends on the context. Did they teach 10,000 last year? If so, what happened this year that caused such a precipitous drop? The numbers alone don't tell the whole story: otherwise, the results might always suggest that more is better and less is bad. Perhaps your liaison program held the highest number of research consultations this year, but at the individual level, you notice that one or two liaisons are carrying that load by themselves, or maybe despite the high numbers, your user surveys show that the consultations aren't perceived as very useful.

Balancing Workloads and Responsibilities

In any evaluation of the individual liaison, be cognizant of other assignments or commitments the liaison may have, whether assigned by you, your supervisor, or others in the institution. Maybe instruction or research consultation stats have dropped because of a big committee assignment. Often there are institutional goals, like increasing instruction, and it might be easy to jump to the conclusion that, therefore, every liaison needs to increase their teaching; it's really important to balance the shared goals of the program with the individual's responsibilities, assignments, skills, and personality. For extroverted liaisons who've been at the institution for decades, networking, connections, and the ensuing results may come easily. For an introverted liaison who's new to this work and to your particular institutional environment, it may be more of an uphill marathon.

Models for Assessment of Liaisons and Liaison Programs

There are a number of models for assessment of liaisons in the literature. We strongly encourage you to review these and consider how they might help you design similar tools for use at your institution. Eric Resnis and Jennifer Natale's article, "Demonstrating Library Impact: Liaison Assessment," includes an effective rubric focused on engagement of liaisons in various arenas and establishes benchmarks for introductory, developing, and advanced levels of engagement.[4]

Be sensitive to the variations you'll see among the liaisons and look for ways to help each of them take positive steps toward the established goals. Look for achievable, easy wins or payoffs tailored to the individual. It's easy to fall into the trap of using your assessment metrics as a yardstick to compare one liaison to another and then grade them on the curve: Liaison A did the most of x, so A gets 100 percent and Liaison B did half that much, so B get a 50 percent. Think of the things you discover in the results as tools for a journey. These metrics can provide the lantern to light the path in front of you as well as the other tools you might need to carry for different tasks along the way, including a map of where you want to go.

Each liaison will likely need to focus on different areas for improvement. Encourage liaisons to reflect on their assignments or departments and develop a plan for how they will meet the needs of the department and its faculty and students. Each liaison should develop SMART goals—goals that are specific, measurable, achievable, relevant, and time bound. Make plans to meet regularly with liaisons to see how they're doing on these goals. It's important to take advantage of opportunities for informal meetings or periodic check-ins to supplement any formal review meetings so that you can adjust plans or offer additional support as needed.

For individual liaisons and for entire liaison programs, the metrics and the narrative these metrics support are crucial for demonstrating the value and influence of liaison work. Often, the most powerful demonstration of influence comes from constituent feedback. We've mentioned earlier instruments such as instruction session feedback from students or post–research consultation follow-up surveys. Another example that can provide even broader assessment of engaged liaison work is surveying the faculty served. Jonathan Miller, in his article "A Method for Evaluating Library Liaison Activities in Small Academic Libraries," discusses an instrument developed for use at his institution designed to help individual liaisons in the creation of a reflective self-evaluation as well as to draft a liaison plan for the next two years.[5] The assessment instrument, which is included in the article, asks faculty members to identify their department, academic rank, how long they've been at the institution, their librarian's name (from a drop down list that includes "I don't know"), the variety of ways in which they've interacted with their librarian, an overall rating of their interactions, and desired amount of interaction. There are several open-ended comment boxes in the survey. It's important to add here that the report provided to each liaison has identifying data removed so as not to compromise the identity of the respondents.

◎ Further Reading

When you're ready to deep-dive assessment and evaluation of your liaison program, you will definitely want to spend some quality time with *Assessing Liaison Librarians: Docu-*

menting Impact for Positive Change, published by the Association of College and Research Libraries.[6] Not only does this book provide an excellent introduction to assessment in libraries in the context of higher education (introduction and chapter 1), it also provides detailed chapters addressing overarching, programmatic assessment (chapter 2) and chapters devoted to various areas of liaison work, including:

- "Assessment of Teaching, Learning, and Literacies"
- "Library Assessment for Online, Blended, and Other Learning Environments"
- "Beyond the Bibliographer: Assessing Collection Development Activities in the New Digital Library"
- "Liaison Librarians and Scholarly Communication: A Framework and Strategies for Assessment"

The final section of the book discusses design and implementation of an overall liaison assessment program, noting that, although "[d]esigning such an assessment program can be a daunting task, the single best advice is to start small and start immediately."[7] Editor and author Daniel C. Mack goes on to offer excellent advice on exactly how to follow this advice, including this important steps:

- Target programs or activities to assess.
- Identify persons to participate in assessment.
- Communicate about the assessment program widely throughout the library.
- Identify relevant assessment tools, measures, and practices relevant to the programs or services that the library plans to assess.
- Establish a timetable for assessment.
- Provide personnel with training and support for conducting assessment.
- Report on results of assessment both internally and externally.
- Incorporate assessment into professional development, annual reviews, modification of existing library programs, and creation of new services.[8]

If you're leading liaisons, you'll definitely want to absorb all this book has to offer, but we want to highlight a few other sections that will be crucial for growing and sustaining a successful program for engaged liaisons. Chapter 7 is all about assessing outreach and engagement. The chapter concludes with an "Individual and Programmatic Assessment Matrix for Outreach and Engagement" that offers great examples of questions and indicators for exploring informal and formal methods of gathering qualitative and quantitative data to assess the work of the liaison program and the individual liaisons. Chapter 8 focuses on the professional development of liaison librarians, specifically the skills relevant to liaisons in the twenty-first century. This chapter includes rubrics for expectations and for organizational and individual activities related to each area of liaison work.

For some, the thought of assessing and evaluating might conjure up scary memories of a final exam for which you weren't prepared or some other judgment day imagery. However, perhaps a better image might be to think of a trip and the tools you'll need for that trip. Imagine you're driving a car to a new, far-away destination. You'll want to make sure the car is in working order, assessing its road-worthiness. Are the tires in good shape? Is the battery charged? Along the journey, you'll use other assessment an evaluation tools, like the fuel gauge and the engine temperature gage, to know when you need to stop and refuel. You'll use GPS or a map to know if you're on course or not and distance and a clock will allow you to anticipate when you'll arrive at your destination. Think of all the aspects of assessment and evaluation as similar tools to help you plan and to know if you're on target to reach your goal. These tools also help us know how to recalibrate as needed (like stopping for gas or auto service). Just like you shouldn't jump in your car and head off without gathering and paying attention to the tools that assist you with the hope that you'll make it to somewhere, you don't want to approach the liaison journey that way either. That would be like not knowing what the goals were, not providing or using the tools to help us assess, and waiting until the annual review to see if we made it or not. In the end, remember that the goal is to successfully arrive at our destination.

◉ Key Points

- Understand the difference between assessment and evaluation.
- Identify all the ways relevant data is currently collected.
- Establish or clarify desired outcomes that align with organizational and institutional goals.
- Identify the process for assessing outcomes.
- Create and document a plan for assessment and evaluation of your liaison program that will also be the basis of assessment and evaluation for individual liaisons.
- Plan to review regularly with liaisons.

◉ Notes

1. Daniel C. Mack and Gary W. White, eds., *Assessing Liaison Librarians: Documenting Impact for Positive Change*, Publications in Librarianship 67 (Chicago: Association of College and Research Libraries, 2014).

2. Eric Resnis and Jennifer Natale, "Demonstrating Library Impact: Liaison Assessment," *The Journal of Academic Librarianship* 46, no. 4 (July 1, 2020): 102158, https://doi.org/10.1016/j.acalib.2020.102158.

3. "Assessment and Evaluation for Continuing and Higher Learning," Certification Academy, accessed October 25, 2020, https://certificationacademy.com/resources/assesment-and-evaluation-for-learning/.

4. Resnis and Natale, "Demonstrating Library Impact."

5. Jonathan Miller, "A Method for Evaluating Library Liaison Activities in Small Academic Libraries," *Journal of Library Administration* 54, no. 6 (August 18, 2014): 483–500, https://doi.org/10.1080/01930826.2014.953387.

6. Mack and White, *Assessing Liaison Librarians*.

7. Daniel C. Mack, "Designing and Implementing a Liaison Assessment Program," in *Assessing Liaison Librarians Documenting Impact for Positive Change*, ed. Daniel C. Mack and Gary W. White, Publications in Librarianship 67 (Chicago: Association of College and Research Libraries, 2014), 139.

8. Mack, "Designing and Implementing a Liaison Assessment Program," 141–43.

Bibliography

"2019 Altmetric Research Grant Winners to Investigate Altmetrics for Creative and Performing Arts Research." *Altmetric* (blog). June 26, 2019. https://www.altmetric.com/press/press -releases/2019-grant-arts-research/.

Abbott, Alison, David Cyranoski, Nicola Jones, Brendan Maher, Quirin Schiermeier, and Richard Van Noorden. "Metrics: Do Metrics Matter?" *Nature* 465, no. 7300 (June 1, 2010): 860–62. https://doi.org/10.1038/465860a.

"Academia.Edu—About." Academia.edu. Accessed February 8, 2020. https://www.academia.edu /about.

American Library Association. "Principles and Strategies for the Reform of Scholarly Communication 1." Association of College and Research Libraries, September 1, 2006. http://www.ala .org/acrl/publications/whitepapers/principlesstrategies.

———. "Professional Ethics." Tools, Publications and Resources, May 19, 2017. http://www.ala .org/tools/ethics.

"Assessment and Evaluation for Continuing and Higher Learning." Certification Academy. Accessed October 25, 2020. https://certificationacademy.com/resources/assesment-and-eval uation-for-learning/.

Bailey, Jason. "New Data Shows Why Van Gogh Changed His Color Palette." Artnome, December 24, 2018. https://www.artnome.com/news/2018/11/26/new-data-shows-why-van-gogh -changed-his-color-palette-to-bright-yellow.

Bales, John G. "Making All the Right Moves for Liaison Engagement: A Strategy for Relating to Faculty." *College & Research Libraries News* 76, no. 10 (2015): 550–51. https://doi.org /10.5860/crln.76.10.9400.

Barone, Tom, and Elliot W. Eisner. *Arts Based Research*, 1st ed. Los Angeles: Sage, 2011.

Bellet, P. S., and M. J. Maloney. "The Importance of Empathy as an Interviewing Skill in Medicine." *JAMA: The Journal of the American Medical Association* 266, no. 13 (1991): 1831–1832. https://doi.org/10.1001/jama.266.13.1831.

Blankstein, Melissa, and Christine Wolff-Eisenberg. "Ithaka S+R US Faculty Survey 2018." Ithaka S+R, April 12, 2019. https://doi.org/10.18665/sr.311199.

Bod, Rens. *A New History of the Humanities: The Search for Principles and Patterns from Antiquity to the Present*. Oxford: Oxford University Press, 2013. https://www.oxfordscholarship.com /view/10.1093/acprof:oso/9780199665211.001.0001/acprof-9780199665211.

Campbell, Jerry D. "Shaking the Conceptual Foundations of Reference: A Perspective." *Reference Services Review* 20, no. 4 (1992): 29–35. https://doi.org/10.1108/eb049164.

Candy, Linda, and Ernest Edmonds. "Practice-Based Research in the Creative Arts: Foundations and Futures from the Front Line." *Leonardo (Oxford)* 51, no. 1 (2018): 63–69. https://doi.org/10.1162/LEON_a_01471.

Carlson, K., T. Schiphorst, and C. Shaw. "ActionPlot: A Visualization Tool for Contemporary Dance Analysis." In *Proceedings of the International Symposium on Computational Aesthetics in Graphics, Visualization, and Imaging—CAe '11*, 113. Vancouver, British Columbia, Canada: ACM Press, 2011. https://doi.org/10.1145/2030441.2030466.

Carroll, Alexander J., Honora N. Eskridge, and Bertha P. Chang. "Lab-Integrated Librarians: A Model for Research Engagement." *College & Research Libraries* 81, no. 1 (2020). https://doi.org/10.5860/crl.81.1.8.

Center for Creative Leadership. "Use Active Listening Skills When Coaching Others." Accessed October 24, 2020. https://www.ccl.org/articles/leading-effectively-articles/coaching-others-use-active-listening-skills/.

Chilvers, Ian, ed. "Fine Arts." In *The Oxford Dictionary of Art and Artists*. Oxford Reference Online. Oxford: Oxford University Press, 2015.

Clarke, Rachel Ivy, and Young-In Kim. "The More Things Change, the More They Stay the Same: Educational and Disciplinary Backgrounds of American Librarians, 1950–2015." *Journal of Education for Library and Information Science* 59, no. 4 (October 2018): 179–205. https://doi.org/10.3138/jelis.59.4.2018-0001.

Colman, Andrew M., ed. "Emotional Intelligence." In *A Dictionary of Psychology*. Oxford Reference Online. Oxford: Oxford University Press, 2015.

Cooper, Danielle, and Roger Schonfeld. "Rethinking Liaison Programs for the Humanities." Ithaka S+R, July 26, 2017. https://doi.org/10.18665/sr.304124.

Corrall, Sheila. "Roles and Responsibilities: Libraries, Librarians and Data." In *Managing Research Data*, edited by Graham Pryor, 105–133. London: Facet, 2012.

Corti, Louise. "Re-Using Archived Qualitative Data—Where, How, Why?" *Archival Science* 7, no. 1 (March 1, 2007): 37–54. https://doi.org/10.1007/s10502-006-9038-y.

Covey, Stephen R. *The 7 Habits of Highly Effective People*. New York: Simon and Schuster Sound Ideas, 1989.

Crowe, Kathryn. "Student Affairs Connection: Promoting the Library through Co-Curricular Activities." *Collaborative Librarianship* 2, no. 3 (2010): 154–58. https://doi.org/10.29087/2010.2.3.02.

Curty, Renata, Ayoung Yoon, Wei Jeng, and Jian Qin. "Untangling Data Sharing and Reuse in Social Sciences." *Proceedings of the Association for Information Science and Technology* 53, no. 1 (2016): 1–5. https://doi.org/10.1002/pra2.2016.14505301025.

Dahl, Candice C. "Library Liaison with Non-Academic Units: A New Application for a Traditional Model." *Partnership: The Canadian Journal of Library and Information Practice and Research* 2, no. 1 (May 21, 2007). https://doi.org/10.21083/partnership.v2i1.242.

"Data Viz of the Week." Baylor University Libraries, August 29, 2020. https://blogs.baylor.edu/digitalscholarship/data-viz-of-the-week/.

Davis, Marta A., and M. Kathleen Cook. "Implementing a Library Liaison Program." *Collection Management* 20, no. 3–4 (July 15, 1996): 157–65. https://doi.org/10.1300/J105v20n03_14.

Denton, A. Blake. "Academic Library and Athletics Partnerships: A Literature Review on Outreach Strategies and Development Opportunities." *The Southeastern Librarian* 67, no. 2 (2019): 8.

DeSanto, Dan, and Aaron Nichols. "Scholarly Metrics Baseline: A Survey of Faculty Knowledge, Use, and Opinion about Scholarly Metrics." *College & Research Libraries* 78, no. 2 (2017). https://doi.org/10.5860/crl.78.2.150.

Díaz, José O., and Meris A. Mandernach. "Relationship Building One Step at a Time: Case Studies of Successful Faculty-Librarian Partnerships." *Portal: Libraries and the Academy* 17, no. 2 (2017): 273–82. https://doi.org/10.1353/pla.2017.0016.

"Digital Humanities." *Wikipedia*, February 13, 2020. https://en.wikipedia.org/w/index.php ?title=Digital_humanities&oldid=940570346.

"Digital Scholarship." Baylor University Libraries. Accessed October 29, 2020. https://blogs.bay lor.edu/digitalscholarship/.

Dweck, Carol S. *Mindset: The New Psychology of Success*, illustrated edition. New York: Random House, 2006.

Elkins, James, ed. *Visual Literacy*, 1st ed. New York: Routledge, 2007.

Elliott, Christine, Marie Rose, and Jolanda-Pieta van Arnhem, eds. *Augmented and Virtual Reality in Libraries*. Library Information Technology Association (LITA) Guides. Lanham: Rowman & Littlefield, 2018.

Ellis, David. "A Behavioural Approach to Information Retrieval System Design." *Journal of Documentation*, 1989.

"Empathy: How Do I Cultivate It?" *Greater Good*. Accessed October 24, 2020. https://greater good.berkeley.edu/topic/empathy/definition.

Fearon, David Jr., Betsy Gunia, Sherry Lake, Barbara E. Pralle, and Andrew L. Sallans. *Research Data Management Services*. SPEC Kit 334, 2013. https://publications.arl.org/Research -Data-Management-Services-SPEC-Kit-334/.

Filgo, Ellen Hampton. "Systematically Understanding Faculty Needs: Using Zotero in Liaison Work." *College & Research Libraries News* 77, no. 1 (January 1, 2016): 18–22.

Fitzgerald, Sarah Rose. "Serving a Fragmented Field: Information Seeking in Higher Education." *The Journal of Academic Librarianship* 44, no. 3 (May 1, 2018): 337–42. https://doi .org/10.1016/j.acalib.2018.03.007.

Folster, Mary B. "A Study of the Use of Information by Social Science Researchers." *Journal of Academic Librarianship* 15, no. 1 (March 1989): 7.

———. "Information Seeking Patterns: Social Sciences." *The Reference Librarian* 23, no. 49–50 (1995): 83–93.

Ford, Barbara J. "Reference beyond (and without) the Reference Desk." *College and Research Libraries* 47, no. 5 (1986): 491–494.

Frank, Donald G., Gregory K. Raschke, Julie Wood, and Julie Z. Yang. "Information Consulting: The Key to Success in Academic Libraries." *The Journal of Academic Librarianship* 27, no. 2 (March 1, 2001): 90–96. https://doi.org/10.1016/S0099-1333(00)00180-4.

Frederick, Jennifer K., and Christine Wolff-Eisenberg. "Ithaka S+R US Library Survey 2019." Ithaka S+R, April 2, 2020.

GitHub.com. "GitHub." Accessed February 8, 2020. https://github.com.

Glynn, Tom, and Connie Wu. "New Roles and Opportunities for Academic Library Liaisons: A Survey and Recommendations." *Reference Services Review* 31, no. 2 (January 1, 2003): 122–28. https://doi.org/10.1108/00907320310476594.

Google Scholar. "About Google Scholar." Accessed February 8, 2020. https://scholar.google.com /intl/en/scholar/about.html.

Hahn, Karla. "Introduction: Positioning Liaison Librarians for the 21st Century." *Research Library Issues: A Bimonthly Report from ARL, CNI, and SPARC*, no. 265 (August 2009): 1–2.

Harris, Valerie A., and Ann C. Weller. "Use of Special Collections as an Opportunity for Outreach in the Academic Library." *Journal of Library Administration* 52, no. 3–4 (2012): 294–303. https://doi.org/10.1080/01930826.2012.684508.

Hemminger, Bradley M., Dihui Lu, K. T. L. Vaughan, and Stephanie J. Adams. "Information Seeking Behavior of Academic Scientists." *Journal of the American Society for Information Science & Technology* 58, no. 14 (December 2007): 2205–25. https://doi.org/10.1002/asi.20686.

Hendrix, Carla A. "Developing a Liaison Program in a New Organizational Structure—A Work in Progress." *Reference Librarian* 32, no. 67/68 (February 28, 2000): 203–24. https://doi .org/10.1300/J120v32n67_15.

Hernon, Peter, and Charles R. McClure. "Unobtrusive Reference Testing: The 55 Percent Rule." *Library Journal* 111, no. 7 (1986): 37–41.

Hitchcock, Julia. "A Contemporary Altarpiece for Our Techno-Human Age." Department of Art and Art History at Baylor University, October 25, 2016. https://www.baylor.edu/art/news .php?action=story&story=177189.

"Humanities." *Wikipedia*, February 5, 2020. https://en.wikipedia.org/w/index.php?title=Human ities&oldid=939203973.

Jaguszewski, Janice M., and Karen Williams. "New Roles for New Times: Transforming Liaison Roles in Research Libraries." Association of Research Libraries, August 2013. http://www.arl .org/publications-resources/2893-new-roles-for-new-times-transforming-liaison-roles-in -research-libraries.

Jeanes, Emma, ed. "Emotional Intelligence." In *A Dictionary of Organizational Behaviour*. Oxford University Press, January 24, 2019. https://www.oxfordreference.com/view/10.1093 /acref/9780191843273.001.0001/acref-9780191843273.

Johnson, Anna Marie. "Connections, Conversations, and Visibility: How the Work of Academic Reference and Liaison Librarians Is Evolving." *Reference & User Services Quarterly* 58, no. 2 (January 18, 2019): 91–102. https://doi.org/10.5860/rusq.58.2.6929.

Kelly, Michael, ed. "Decorative Arts." In *Encyclopedia of Aesthetics*. Oxford Reference Online. New York: Oxford University Press, 2014.

Kennedy, Marie, and Kristine Brancolini. "Academic Librarian Research: A Survey of Attitudes, Involvement, and Perceived Capabilities." *College and Research Libraries* 73, no. 5 (2012): 431–48.

Kenney, Anne R. "Leveraging the Liaison Model: From Defining 21st Century Research Libraries to Implementing 21st Century Research Universities." Ithaka S+R, March 25, 2014. http://www.sr.ithaka.org/blog/leveraging-the-liaison-model-from-defining-21st-century -research-libraries-to-implementing-21st-century-research-universities/.

Klaus, Peggy. *The Hard Truth about Soft Skills: Workplace Lessons Smart People Wish They'd Learned Sooner*, 1st ed. New York: HarperCollins, 2007.

Klein, Gary. "Mindsets: What They Are and Why They Matter." *Psychology Today*, May 1, 2016. https://www.psychologytoday.com/blog/seeing-what-others-dont/201605/mindsets.

Kuh, George D., Ty M. Cruce, Rick Shoup, Jillian Kinzie, and Robert M. Gonyea. "Unmasking the Effects of Student Engagement on First-Year College Grades and Persistence." *The Journal of Higher Education* 79, no. 5 (September 2008): 540–63. https://doi.org/10.1080/00221 546.2008.11772116.

Lagasse, Paul. "Science." *The Columbia Encyclopedia*. New York: Columbia University Press, August 1, 2018. http://search.credoreference.com/content/entry/columency/social_science/0.

———. "Social Science." *The Columbia Encyclopedia*. New York: Columbia University Press, August 1, 2018. http://search.credoreference.com/content/entry/columency/social_science/0.

Lampert, Lynn D., Katherine S. Dabbour, and Jacqueline Solis. "When It's All Greek: The Importance of Collaborative Information Literacy Outreach Programming to Greek Student Organizations." *Research Strategies* 20, no. 4 (January 1, 2005): 300–310. https://doi.org/10.1016 /j.resstr.2006.12.005.

Latta, Gail F. *Liaison Services in ARL Libraries. SPEC Kit 189*. Association of Research Libraries, 1992.

LeMire, Sarah, Stephanie J. Graves, Sean Buckner, Donald D. Freeman, and Gerald L. Smith. "Basic Training: A Library Orientation Designed for Student Veterans." *The Journal of Academic Librarianship* 46, no. 4 (July 1, 2020): 102137. https://doi.org/10.1016/j.acalib.2020.102137.

Liaison with Users Committee, Collection Development and Evaluation Section, and Reference and Adult Services Division. "Guidelines for Liaison Work." *RQ* 32, no. 2 (1992): 198–204.

Liaison with Users Committee, Collection Development and Evaluation Section, and Reference and User Services Association. "Guidelines for Liaison Work in Managing Collections and Services." Reference & User Services Association (RUSA), 2009. http://www.ala.org/rusa /resources/guidelines/guidelinesliaison.

Line, Maurice B. "The Information Uses and Needs of Social Scientists: An Overview of INFROSS." *ASLIB Proceedings; London* 23, no. 8 (August 1, 1971): 412.

LinkedIn.com. "About LinkedIn." Accessed February 8, 2020. https://about.linkedin.com/.

Logue, Susan, John Ballestro, Andrea Imre, and Julie Arendt. "Liaison Services, SPEC Kit 301 (October 2007)," Association of Research Libraries, October 1, 2007. https://publications.arl.org/Liaison-Services-SPEC-Kit-301/.

Love, Emily. "Building Bridges: Cultivating Partnerships between Libraries and Minority Student Services." *Education Libraries* 30, no. 1 (September 5, 2017): 13. https://doi.org/10.26443/el.v30i1.232.

Love, Emily, and Margaret B. Edwards. "Forging Inroads between Libraries and Academic, Multicultural and Student Services." *Reference Services Review* 37, no. 1 (January 1, 2009): 20–29. https://doi.org/10.1108/00907320910934968.

Luo, Lili. "Fusing Research into Practice: The Role of Research Methods Education." *Library & Information Science Research* 33, no. 3 (July 1, 2011): 191–201. https://doi.org/10.1016/j.lisr.2010.12.001.

Mack, Daniel C. "Beyond the Bibliographer: Assessing Collection Development Activities in the New Digital Library." In *Assessing Liaison Librarians Documenting Impact for Positive Change*, edited by Daniel C. Mack and Gary W. White. Publications in Librarianship 67. Chicago: Association of College and Research Libraries, 2014.

———. "Designing and Implementing a Liaison Assessment Program." In *Assessing Liaison Librarians Documenting Impact for Positive Change*, edited by Daniel C. Mack and Gary W. White. Publications in Librarianship 67. Chicago: Association of College and Research Libraries, 2014.

Mack, Daniel C., and Gary W. White, eds. *Assessing Liaison Librarians Documenting Impact for Positive Change*. Publications in Librarianship 67. Chicago: Association of College and Research Libraries, 2014.

Malone, Andrea. "From Liaison to Coordinator: How Digital Humanities Influenced a Role Change and Restructure." In *Academic Librarian in the Digital Age: Essays on Changing Roles and Responsibilities*, edited by Tom Diamond. Jefferson, NC: McFarland, 2020.

Mann, Charles Riborg. *A Study of Engineering Education: Prepared for the Joint Committee on Engineering Education of the National Engineering Societies*. Massachusetts: Merrymount Press, 1918. https://hdl.handle.net/2027/wu.89077496529.

Marsalis, Scott, and Julia A. Kelly. "Building a RefWorks Database of Faculty Publications as a Liaison and Collection Development Tool." *Issues in Science and Technology Librarianship* 40, Summer 2004. http://conservancy.umn.edu/handle/11299/42227.

May, Sandra. "Engineering Design Process." NASA, July 17, 2017. http://www.nasa.gov/audience/foreducators/best/edp.html.

McLeish, Kenneth, ed. "Profession." In *Bloomsbury Guide to Human Thought*. Bloomsbury, 1993.

Meho, Lokman I., and Helen R. Tibbo. "Modeling the Information-Seeking Behavior of Social Scientists: Ellis's Study Revisited." *Journal of the American Society for Information Science and Technology* 54, no. 6 (2003): 570–87. https://doi.org/10.1002/asi.10244.

"Mendeley Database." Elsevier Solutions. Accessed February 8, 2020. https://www.elsevier.com/solutions/mendeley.

Merriam-Webster. "Agile." Accessed October 24, 2020. https://www.merriam-webster.com/dictionary/agile.

———. "Flexible." Accessed October 24, 2020. https://www.merriam-webster.com/dictionary/flexible.

Meyer, Erin E. "Low-Hanging Fruit: Leveraging Short-Term Partnerships to Advance Academic Library Outreach Goals." *Collaborative Librarianship* 6, no. 3 (2014): 10.

Miebach, Nathalie. *Art Made of Storms*. TEDGlobal 2011, 2011. https://www.ted.com/talks/nathalie_miebach_art_made_of_storms.

Miller, Jonathan. "A Method for Evaluating Library Liaison Activities in Small Academic Libraries." *Journal of Library Administration* 54, no. 6 (August 18, 2014): 483–500. https://doi.org/10.1080/01930826.2014.953387.

Miller, Laurence. "Liaison Work in the Academic Library." *RQ* 16, no. 3 (April 1, 1977): 213–15.

Miller, Rebecca K., and Lauren Pressley. "Evolution of Library Liaisons, SPEC Kit 349," Association of Research Libraries, November 3, 2015. http://publications.arl.org/Evolution-Library-Liaisons-SPEC-Kit-349/.

Miller, William. "What's Wrong with Reference: Coping with Success and Failure at the Reference Desk." *American Libraries* 15, no. 5 (May 1984): 303–22.

Murphy, Sarah Anne, and Craig Gibson. "Informing the Evolution of an Engaged Liaison Librarian Model." In *Assessing Liaison Librarians Documenting Impact for Positive Change*, edited by Daniel C. Mack and Gary W. White. Publications in Librarianship 67. Chicago: Association of College and Research Libraries, 2014.

Musick Peery, Katie, Morgan Chivers, and Tara Radniecki. "Maker Competencies and the Undergraduate Curriculum." Presented at the International Symposium on Academic Makerspaces, Stanford, CA, August 4, 2018. http://hdl.handle.net/10106/27653.

Nero, Neil, and Anne Langley. "Subject Liaisons in Academic Libraries: An Open Access Data Set from 2015." *Portal: Libraries and the Academy* 17, no. 1 (2017): 5–15. https://doi.org/10.1353/pla.2017.0001.

Nicholas, David, Cherifa Boukacem-Zeghmouri, Blanca Rodríguez-Bravo, Jie Xu, Anthony Watkinson, A. Abrizah, Eti Herman, and Marzena Świgoń. "Where and How Early Career Researchers Find Scholarly Information." *Learned Publishing* 30, no. 1 (2017): 19–29. https://doi.org/10.1002/leap.1087.

Oakleaf, Megan. "The Value of Academic Libraries: A Comprehensive Research Review and Report." Chicago: Association of College and Research Libraries, American Library Association, 2010.

Onorato, Mary, Rebecca Springer, Amanda L. Watson, John Tofanelli, Matthew Roberts, Ashley Champagne, Darby Fanning, and Julie Frick Wade. "What Is Humanities Research Now?" MLA, 2020. https://mla.confex.com/mla/2020/meetingapp.cgi/Session/6465.

Owens, Tammi M., and Katie Bishop. "'Let's Try It!': Library Outreach in a Culture of Yes." *Public Services Quarterly* 14, no. 1 (February 14, 2018): 75–82. https://doi.org/10.1080/15228959.2017.1411861.

Palumbo, Laura Bolton, Jeffra D. Bussmann, and Barbara Kern. "The Value of Subject Specialization and the Future of Science Liaison Librarianship." *College and Research Libraries*, 2021. https://doi.org/10.7282/T3-6B34-DK85.

Pentassuglia, Monica. "'The Art(Ist) Is Present': Arts-Based Research Perspective in Educational Research." *Cogent Education* 4, no. 1 (2017). https://doi.org/10.1080/2331186x.2017.1301011.

ResearchGate.com. "ResearchGate—About." Accessed February 8, 2020. https://www.researchgate.net/about.

Resnis, Eric, and Jennifer Natale. "Demonstrating Library Impact: Liaison Assessment." *The Journal of Academic Librarianship* 46, no. 4 (July 1, 2020): 102158. https://doi.org/10.1016/j.acalib.2020.102158.

Ryans, Cynthia C., Raghini S. Suresh, and Wei-Ping Zhang. "Assessing an Academic Library Liaison Programme." *Library Review* 44, no. 1 (February 1995): 14–23. https://doi.org/10.1108/00242539510076961.

"Science, Technology, Engineering, and Mathematics." *Wikipedia*, April 26, 2020. https://en.wikipedia.org/w/index.php?title=Science,_technology,_engineering,_and_mathematics&oldid=953201346.

"Scientific Method." *Wikipedia*, April 28, 2020. https://en.wikipedia.org/w/index.php?title=Scientific_method&oldid=953701752.

Seamans, Nancy H., and Paul Metz. "Virginia Tech's Innovative College Librarian Program." *College and Research Libraries* 63, no. 4 (July 2002): 324–32.

Serafini, Frank. *Reading the Visual: An Introduction to Teaching Multimodal Literacy.* New York: Teachers College Press, 2013.

"Social Science." *Wikipedia*, February 24, 2020. https://en.wikipedia.org/w/index.php?title =Social_science&oldid=942401311.

Steely, Adrienne. "'Cycles' for Full Orchestra and Electronics." Thesis, Baylor University, 2016. https://baylor-ir.tdl.org/handle/2104/9915.

Stelmaszak, Marta, and Philipp Hukal. "When Data Science Meets Social Sciences: The Benefits of the Data Revolution Are Clear but Careful Reflection Is Needed." *Impact of Social Sciences* (blog), March 1, 2017. https://blogs.lse.ac.uk/impactofsocialsciences/2017/03/01/when -data-science-meets-social-sciences-the-benefits-of-the-data-revolution-are-clear-but-care ful-reflection-is-needed/.

Stoan, Stephen K. "Research and Information Retrieval among Academic Researchers: Implications for Library Instruction." *Library Trends* 39, no. 3 (1991): 238–57.

Stoddart, Richard A., Thedis W. Bryant, Amia L. Baker, Adrienne Lee, and Brett Spencer. "Going Boldly beyond the Reference Desk: Practical Advice and Learning Plans for New Reference Librarians Performing Liaison Work." *The Journal of Academic Librarianship* 32, no. 4 (July 2006): 419–27. https://doi.org/10.1016/j.acalib.2006.03.009.

Strothmann, Molly, and Karen Antell. "The Live-In Librarian: Developing Library Outreach to University Residence Halls." *Reference & User Services Quarterly* 50, no. 1 (2010): 48–58.

Swartz, Pauline S., Brian A. Carlisle, and E. Chisato Uyeki. "Libraries and Student Affairs: Partners for Student Success." *Reference Services Review* 35, no. 1 (January 1, 2007): 109–22. https://doi.org/10.1108/00907320710729409.

Todorinova, Lily. "A Mixed-Method Study of Undergraduate and First Year Librarian Positions in Academic Libraries in the United States." *The Journal of Academic Librarianship* 44, no. 2 (March 1, 2018): 207–15. https://doi.org/10.1016/j.acalib.2018.02.005.

———. "Listening as Leadership." *Baylor University Human Resources: Learn and Lead*, n.d.

Towers, Sha, Ellen Hampton Filgo, Eileen M. Bentsen, Christina Y. Chan-Park, Clayton E. Crenshaw, Ben Johansen, Megan Martinsen, et al. "Liaison Framework for the Research and Engagement Librarians of Baylor University." Working Paper. Accessed November 9, 2020. https://hdl.handle.net/2104/11086.

Tyckoson, David A. "Issues and Trends in the Management of Reference Services: A Historical Perspective." *Journal of Library Administration* 51, no. 3 (March 24, 2011): 259–78. https:// doi.org/10.1080/01930826.2011.556936.

Vozza, Stephanie. "6 Ways to Become a Better Listener." *Fast Company*, March 17, 2017. https:// www.fastcompany.com/3068959/6-ways-to-become-a-better-listener.

Wainwright, Amy, and Chris Davidson. "Academic Libraries and Non-Academic Departments: A Survey and Case Studies on Liaising Outside the Box." *Collaborative Librarianship* 9, no. 2 (2017): 19.

Whatley, Kara M. "New Roles of Liaison Librarians: A Liaison's Perspective." *Research Library Issues: A Bimonthly Report from ARL, CNI, and SPARC*, no. 256 (August 31, 2009): 29–32.

Williams, Karen. "A Framework for Articulating New Library Roles." *Research Library Issues: A Bimonthly Report from ARL, CNI, and SPARC*, no. 265 (August 31, 2009): 4–8.

Wilson, Myoung C. "Evolution or Entropy? Changing Reference/User Culture and the Future of Reference Librarians." *Reference & User Services Quarterly* 39, no. 4 (2000): 387–90.

Wolff, Christine, Alisa B Rod, and Roger C Schonfeld. "Ithaka S+R US Faculty Survey 2015," 2015, 83.

Index

About the Authors

Ellen Hampton Filgo is the director of the Liaison Program for the Baylor University Libraries. As such, she provides administrative leadership over the liaison librarian program in the Research and Engagement department, managing a team of liaisons who reach out to and engage with their assigned schools, departments, and major programs on campus to provide high quality and effective research, information literacy, collections, and scholarly communication services. She is also the liaison to the departments of Modern Languages and Cultures; Communication; Film and Digital Media; and Journalism, Public Relations, and New Media. She received her BA in comparative literature from Oberlin College and her master's in library science from the University of North Carolina at Chapel Hill. Outside of her job, she loves Anglican theology, Balkan history and politics, reading long-form journalism, checking things off of her baking bucket list, and spending time with her husband and two boys.

Sha Towers is the associate dean for Research and Engagement in the Baylor University Libraries, leading a team of directors who oversee the liaison program, public services, instruction and information literacy, special collections, and data and digital scholarship. He holds the master of Library and Information Science degree from the University of Texas and the master of Music History and Literature degree from Baylor University. He is a 2011 cohort member of the Harvard Leadership Institute for Academic Librarians and in 2018 was promoted to the highest rank of faculty librarians at Baylor University. Towers served as the head of the fine arts library at Baylor for nine years, during which time he developed a new model of librarian engagement with the faculty and students in the arts fields. As a result of this work, he was invited to lead the reference department in a major reorganization with the goal of transitioning the reference librarians to a more proactive liaison model, a program he led from 2012 until 2019. He currently serves as the liaison to the departments of Theatre and Art and Art History. Sha is also a practicing artist in music, calligraphy, and book arts. He enjoys spending time with his wife, two sons, and two Great Danes.